Living the Legend
The Journal of a Titanic Background Actress

Judy Prestininzi

Copyright © 2012 Judy Prestininzi
All Rights Reserved

ISBN: 1475185286
ISBN-13: 9781475185287

I dedicate this journal to my children:
Jeff Anthony Prestininzi
Craig Dominic Prestininzi
Daughter-in-law
Francine Jacqueline Prestininzi
I love you all so very much, I hope you will always remember this and smile.

Living the Legend
The Journal of a Titanic Background Actress

BY JUDY PRESTININZI

Copyright Sept. 22, 1996

Introduction

It was a typical evening back in the spring of 1996. I was going about my usual routine of feeding horses, cats, and family. My older son, Craig, was away at college. He would occasionally call to give me up dates on his studies in architecture. This evening he would call with a bit more than just the usual school and club activities. He had been at work, a print shop on campus, which can be slow and a bit boring at times, especially on a Sunday night. He logged on to the internet and was searching for information about some of his more favorite ships from the past. First he found the *USS Constitution*, then the *Titanic*, which noted that a film directed by James Cameron was in the works. He then proceeded to find Mr. Cameron's website which briefly outlined what he was doing.

When he called me that evening he was excited about what he had discovered. The production was to be done in Rosarito, Mexico, about one and a half hours south of our home in San Marcos, California. My reaction to that location was, "Why down there?" I had been in Rosarito several years before and did not really care for it, but the possibility of working on a film was quite alluring. My son alerted me to a possible casting call to be held in San Diego sometime in the near future. We laughed about the fantasy of being a movie star and the thoughts of working with some of our favorite actors. I told him I would keep an eye open for anything happening here.

Two months passed. It was early June. I was watching a local news station and the casting call was announced. They would be holding it downtown, at the St. James Hotel the following morning at 11 a.m. I informed my family of what was going on and readied myself for this call that had a potential of drawing 2500 people or more. Knowing that parking was hard enough to find on a normal day downtown, I could visualize the potential problems so I arrived two hours early. This was a very wise move on my part. I was able to park close by and was only a half an hour back in line when they opened the doors. As we stood in line, we visited and helped each other take our various body and head measurements that was asked for on our application. That was a sight in itself to most of the people passing by because we were doing this out on the sidewalk in front of the hotel. Being downtown, we also attracted numerous and curious street inhabitants, that thought we were there for free food or housing, and possibly to entertain them. Of course, there were those that wanted to entertain us as well.

Finally getting inside, we were seated at tables to fill out basic résumés on ourselves. The woman in charge was named Amy. We wrote in all of our measurements that we had taken earlier and some of our hobbies, sports, etc., a little about ourselves, family and jobs. After that, we had a picture taken and given a number. The whole thing took about 20 minutes that was it. We were told that if we were selected to be a core member, of which there were to be 150 to 200, we would get a call the first part of August.

Well, August came and went. I hadn't heard a thing, so I thought that I wouldn't be called. Then I heard that production was two months behind. There was still hope that I would get a call, but as mid-September passed, I still had heard nothing. So I just figured that I wasn't going.

On Sunday, September 22, 1996, I was sick in bed with some kind of bug. At 9:45 p.m. I heard the phone ring and I thought it was only a family member since it was so late in the evening. I heard my husband say, "Just a minute." He came to our room saying, "Honey, it's the Titanic!" I sat up in bed and replied, "You're kidding!" I got well real quick. They told me that I had been selected to be in a featured role as "a woman in the gym" and wanted to know if I was interested. "Of course!" I told them, "What would you like me to do?" They wanted me to come to the studio for a fitting on Tuesday, the 24th. I was so excited I couldn't believe it. I was in total shock. Immediately I called my parents and my sons. They were all excited and curious about what was next, but I had no information for them, I only knew that I was going.

My son Craig asked if I knew who was directing. I had no clue (even though he told me a few months ago). He told me that it was going to be James Cameron. I still had no clue. He very firmly told me, "Mom, he only made your most favorite films, like Aliens, Terminator II, and True Lies." I was silent for a moment as this bit of trivia sunk into my tired, numbed, little brain. When reality struck, all I could say was, "You've got to be kidding. Wow, wouldn't that be cool if Arnold was there!" He then informed me that it would be more likely that I would see Bill Paxton first, because he had a role in the film. He also told me that Kathy Bates would be Molly Brown. I could feel the excitement building in my sick little body. I was going to get well by Tuesday!

Tuesday has arrived. Still feeling the last of the effects of what ever was ailing me. I get on I-15 south and head to San Diego. Rush hour as usual is slow and frustrating. As I approach the border, traffic is not as heavy. Crossing is quick and now I need to find my direction before going any farther into unknown territory. They want me to meet a bus at a place called Senior Taco, just the other side of the border. I had a good idea of where it was. They said it was near the Holiday Inn, which turned out to be a good landmark, as it was the tallest building in the area. I spotted it right away, but now I had to find the right roads to get there. That was interesting, because there were a few one way streets that I had to navigate around to get to my destination. I could see Senior Taco two streets over from where I was, but I was still going the opposite direction. As I took a quick look around, I saw the road I needed to be on. Not having a map, I was quite proud of myself. I arrived an hour early. The place looked abandoned and the parking lot was dirt, potholes and rocks. Of course I was the only one there, so I went across the street to a shopping center. There were a variety of little shops and I wandered around all of them. I saw a pet shop that was supposed to be a veterinary clinic as well. I went inside and was absolutely horrified. There were several dead dogs still lying in their cages. One looked like it died a painful death, it stank of death. Sick to my stomach, I hurried out. There are seemingly no rules against animal cruelty in Mexico. I could see the parking lot from where I was and a couple of people had arrived. So I went back over to meet my acting partners. As we were standing around we began to get acquainted. I told them of my experience across the street. They were shocked. It was very interesting meeting all these people. Anna Hilton, who shortly here after I call my "other child," is 17 years old. She went to San Marcos High School, San Marcos, with my sons, Craig and Jeff, but they had never met each other. Debbie Hilton, Anna's mother, works at Palomar College, San Marcos. We find out that we live only 10 minutes away from each other. With great delight I also discover they are Christians and also know some other dear friends of ours, what a small world. Next, I meet Ellen Mower O'Brien, tall and thin, she drives a 1962 Alfa Romero. Her husband works on old cars as we do. She is a medical artist that had worked at UCSD Medical Center, in San Diego. She is also acquainted with my youngest son's neurosurgeon, who had operated on him in August 1995. Trish, another skinny mini from San Diego, she could be a Julia Roberts look-a-like. James, a nurse at one of San Diego's military hospitals. Drew, who could be Scott Bakula's brother. CC Burroughs, has two girls, is a writer, and lives in Escondido, just 15 minutes away from me.

    Now the bus has arrived. Not at all what we would have expected to ride in. Some of the tires are bald, and a big hole in the roof for air-conditioning. We meet Rudy, he is our first contact with the casting crew. He was going to school in Monterey, decided to quit and come down to get a job at the studio. He works hard and has been in a couple of scenes already. I admire this young man for his determination. He has a list of those that are supposed to meet him and checks us in as we board our somewhat unsightly chariot. As we leave, one of the bus drivers remains standing in the open doorway of the bus. We just watch him as we wind our way through Tijuana. We wonder if he will remain there the entire trip. Some of the roads are not what you would call in good repair. We finally reach the highway that leads to Rosarito. He is still standing there as we reach 55-65 mph. Ellen and I being to exchange worried glances, that we may witness an unfortunate accident if we go around one more sharp turn. Well, we joke that there is a nurse on board if something were to happen and that she could draw a picture of it for the local news! In an attempt to ignore the situation, we begin talking about ourselves and our families. I told her of my son, Jeff, who is 21 now, and the brain surgery he had undergone just a year ago. How fortunate we were that we still had him, considering that he still has the cystic lesions in his brain, which caused him to collapse one night. After arriving at the hospital and a CAT scan, the discovery of water compressing his brain, and emergency surgery to relieve pressure, then the discovery of a 1 3/4 inch aneurysm behind his left eye that lead to a 12 hour operation three months later. The painful recovery and that he was doing very well now, but he still has lingering movement problems on his right side and his endurance was very poor. The most amazing thing was that the doctors determined that he had these things since birth and that he had played football and powerlifted for at least six years prior with no outward signs that anything was wrong. Ellen said she had never heard of all those problems in one person before. I told her that neither had the doctors and that he would be entered in the medical journals for it. I also stated that this was not the type of fame I wanted for my child. He had planned on coming with me today, but he had a very bad cold and stayed in bed. Ellen and James, both having a medical background, were very concerned and interested in Jeff's condition. So that was the main topic as we traveled south.

As we entered Rosarito our attentions turned to finding the studio. We had all heard that you could see the *Titanic* sitting on the beach, but we quickly found that it was about three miles south of town and we couldn't see it yet. We traveled through town with that man still standing in the doorway of the bus. We went on overpasses with no guard rails. Saw all the local merchants along the roadside and the sad looking horses that were kept tied and saddled for tourists to ride along the beach. There are a lot of stray dogs in the area because people don't believe in spaying and neutering them, some kind of macho thing I hear. It's very sad to see, because they all are under feed, mangy, and some even crippled from being hit by cars. I think to myself, "Boy, the animal activists would have a fit down here." But no one seems to care because that is their way of life.

As we come up over a little hill, we all get quiet. There she was... *Titanic*! Oh, my goodness. We could not believe what we were seeing. The first glimpse of her was astounding and she wasn't even close to being finished. The funnels are what we see first, 90% scale are their size. Some of us have cameras and capture this stage of construction. As we arrive inside the studio our excitement builds. We pass by construction buildings where almost everything that will be used on the sets and the ship are being made. Fiberglass molds for the lifeboats, wicker furniture, lifeboat davits, prop machinery, another funnel and even the bow of the ship. Everything is under 24 hour construction. We eagerly search for camera crews but soon find out they are working inside. We pass by a group of first class passengers and are quickly amazed at their costume detail. Men in their tuxedos and women in their evening gowns. They had arrived two weeks earlier and were part of the core group. Our bus arrives in front of the casting department and we pile out. We are greeted by Amy Caton-Ford, Kelly McCall and Maggie Jimenez, all nice, but very busy ladies. We are instructed to sit down and fill out some papers. So after that, we wait and a group of women come out with Amy and the others. They begin to look us over and talking amongst themselves. We all feel like livestock on display. They ask all of the women that have long hair to take it down and turn around so they could see it. We hear a bunch of "oos" and "aahs" and they come up to us to feel our hair. We later discover that this was the hair department. The more of us with long hair, the less they would have to use wigs. Then we were asked how many of us could swim? Not knowing what we were about to get into, Ellen, CC, Anna, myself and a whole lot of us raise our hands. With that we begin a waiting game for entering wardrobe. We all start getting a little hungry. They had put a table out with some Mexican sweet bread and sodas, that's all. In one area they had a video running of a very poor version of *The Titanic*, done sometime in the 60's. Finally, after which seemed forever, I get called back for my fitting. They asked me what I had been told my part would be. I told them I was to be featured in the gym. After a little discussion between themselves, I was told that I would not be doing that part and that I was going to be a 3rd class passenger instead of 1st. This happened because I was not tall enough for the size 3 outfit they had originally thought I could wear. I laughed and said that not even in my best day could I fit into a size 3, 5 yes, but not a 3. Amy asked me if I minded the change, all I said was "Is this a good thing that was happening or not?" She just said it was up to me and they needed to know so they could fit me. What could I say but "OK." To the fitting room I went. Lollie, is the lady that took care of me. I got the ugliest, stinkiest outfit. The mildew smell was awful. She said she would have it cleaned before I had to work in it. Then she went and got me a full body wetsuit. I asked what we were getting these for and find out we will be in a three and a half foot deep, heated pool that is about 10,000 square feet in size. If it is heated why did we need wetsuits? Well, it was only heated to 87 degrees and after a few hours in it we would tend to get cold. I had never had a wetsuit on before so I didn't know how it should fit. I was told it should fit snug and so it did. After my fitting, it was back to sitting again, something we would all get use to real fast.

    We started to meet a few people from the core. Rick Courtney, from Canada, looks like an English Bobby. He has been on the production since the beginning in Halifax. He was there when the soup was poisoned with PCP and alerted the paramedics. He is a really nice guy and answers a lot of our questions. Ken Rounds and Ralph Cox, very distinguished looking gentlemen. Ken is from LA and looks like Mr. Monopoly. Ralph lives in Rosarito with his wife Kay, who is also an extra. It was really fun finding out their background and what they had already done on the film.

    It's late afternoon, we are board and hungry. Drew and I decide to go explore the studio. We head to the ship to check it out. It is the upper deck that is being worked on now, we are not sure how long it was at this point. It was suspended over a tank that appeared to be at least 50 feet deep. Later we find out that it is deeper on one end then the other, because they would actually be sinking the front. The tank would hold 17 million gallons of unheated sea water, pumped directly from the ocean nearby. It would take 20 hours with 4 giant pumps and some type of filtering system to fill it. We just could not comprehend what this would look like when it was finished.

Now it's getting late, 8:30 in the evening. We were told we would only be there a couple of hours. No offer of food, everyone is getting edgy. 8:45, on the bus back to T.J. It is cold because of the hole in the roof, glad I brought my jacket. Finally get back home at 11:00 p.m. We discussed killing and eating one of our leaders. Almost had the Donner Party Meets the Titanic! Uhm...good horror plot.

2

September 24, Wednesday

I get a call on Wednesday to come to Tijuana on Thursday for some kind of swim test. I go to Senior Taco again and there are some of the same people that I met on Tuesday. There are also some new faces among us. My son, Jeff came with me today and we brought the video camera so we could record the activities for posterity. Ellen is there and we quickly team up. We get on that same cruddy bus and Rudy is there to guide us once more. We go to some place that looks like an abandoned athletic training facility. The buildings look as if they have been closed up for a while, but there were people jogging on the track. We wind our way through some hallways and arrive in the rear of the facility where we see a pool with a high dive and another large pool that is full of local people. They have reserved the high dive for us and it is about 30 feet high.

    We are met by Simon Crane, stunt coordinator, who also worked with Mel Gibson on Braveheart. I fall in love with his English accent immediately. He tells us what we should expect and what he expects from us. If we don't feel comfortable doing something, then we are to let him know. He doesn't want us to get hurt or endanger someone else. Now we are to go get in our cloths that we are going to swim in. We all are very curious of what is ahead.

    We gather in a circle around Simon and he divides us into a couple of groups. Ellen and I stick together and go to the high dive first. Jeff is off to the side with the camera rolling. We make our way up the narrow staircase in groups of four. There are some stunt people up there waiting for us. They put full body harnesses on each of us and cable it to the steel railing. One of the men takes us one at a time to the edge of the platform. I didn't want to go first, I wanted to see what a couple of others did before I ventured forth. Then it was my turn. The man that helped me harness up was very nice, he was in Braveheart too. He walked me over to the edge and I was holding on to his arm. He told me to look down at the man that was floating around in the pool. I still had a very firm hold of his arm as I looked over the edge. I could feel that my weight was being taken by the harness and felt a little better about being on the edge. He asked me if I was all right and I said "Yes, that I was just not used to being hung out on the edge of something that high up." I felt kind of stupid and I had the giggles, I get like that when I'm nervous and boy was I nervous! Anyway, I was to pretend that the man in the pool was a lifeboat and that they were leaving without me. I was to scream and yell to get their attention so they would come back for me. As I began my routine I noticed that everybody on the ground got quiet and looked up at me. I continued to beg for their return and when I finished I received the applause of all below. Ellen said I had a very good outside voice. I told her that's what you get when you live on a ranch all your life.

    Next, we gather over with Gary Powell, a very large stuntman, that was also in Braveheart. We find that most all of the people that are there, are Simon's stunt crew from England and appeared in Braveheart, but Gary was very prominent in it. Mel Gibson kills him. We are all taken with these people, because we have never been around them before, at least I was and felt like a kid in a candy store. Gary tells me that since I have the biggest mouth that I will be the first to tumble onto the big green mats and into the waiting arms of Simon and James. They were there to keep us from landing wrong and hurting ourselves. We do some shoulder roles, summer salts and landing on our stomachs. When I did the summersaults I got a little dizzy but recovered quickly. It was quite amusing to watch everybody.

Now we are to get into the pool below the high dive. It is 15 feet deep and we can't touch the bottom. This is what Simon is looking for to get an idea of our swimming skills. For our safety there are a couple of divers in diving gear under us if someone goes down. There are also several people around the top of the pool to watch from above. We are to "drowned" for Simon, who is filming us as we do so. We are to panic, scream, grab on to each other and what ever else that comes to our minds if we were trying to save ourselves. We were to remember that it is make believe though and not hurt each other. Some people have on life jackets, some did not. I did not and asked why all the tall people got them. I was put right in the middle of the frenzied group on the first take. I was immediately grabbed, climbed on and over thus being able to see the divers under me. Well, after being mugged to death, I decided to move to the outer edge of the crowd where I could grab and climb. That was much more to my liking. There I did my thrashing and screaming a couple more times. That was it, we were done and the next group entered the torture arena.

We went back to the locker room and changed. We were all laughing at what we had just experienced and wondered what would come of us now. After everyone else was done, we gathered around Simon, who told us that after he views the tape of our swimming we would be notified of our next step. We went back to that bus again and were told that if we were picked for the core swimming group we would know tonight. As we traveled home, Jeff and I discussed whether or not he wanted to try to be in the film. He did, but school was a factor and we didn't know what he might have to do. I told him I would try to find out if he was needed.

That evening, about 9:30 I got a call to come to work on Saturday, the 28th at 5:45 a.m. Anna Hilton got a call too. Her mother called me and told me that she was not called, because she did not want to swim, but would I mind if Anna went with us? I told her there would be no problem at all and that my husband would be going down with us because he had already been to the house where we would be staying. That was great, no worries on anyone. We would leave tomorrow.

We got all packed and hit the road at 8:00 p.m. It was a Friday night and we hit a big traffic jam at the border going into Mexico. It took 45 minutes to get close to the crossing. We are in my old '62 Chevy Impala SS, which has not been running properly and it decides to overheat about 50 yards from the crossing. This is not fun. I turn off the car and we all pile out. It looks like a Chinese fire drill and we all start pushing. The agents see us coming and direct us to the side where we sit and wait for our beast to cool off. We had some water with us and were able to get going after about 20 minutes. Head 'em up and move 'em out, we were on our way.

The house that we would be staying at belonged to our boss, Hart K., in San Diego. It was about 5 miles passed the studio on the free road. We had to get on the toll road to Ensenada and just follow the map he had given us. So far so good, we get off at Rosarito and travel through town towards the studio. Once again we see her, Titanic, even more beautiful at night. I stop, just outside the studio and we all get out and look for a few minutes. Can't wait for tomorrow. Back in the car, we have no trouble finding the house. My husband turns on the gas and water well pump. We unload the car and hit the sack, 4:30 a.m. will come quickly.

3

September 28, Saturday

We drag out of bed and get moving at 4:30 a.m. We arrive at the studio at 5:45. I drive right in, not knowing I should have stopped at the gate, oh well. I go right to the casting office and find out where our parking is. My husband, Craig and son, Jeff, could not stay. Not knowing how long we would be there, I didn't know what to tell them about when to pick us up. There was no phone where we were staying, so all they could do was come back later.

Anna and I go to the women's dressing room where we see some familiar faces. We have different outfits than before. These are called our "drowning clothes." Mine is a black skirt with a long sleeved shirt, dark blue with small white flower print. With wetsuit on, these clothes go over it. Now it's time to go to the hair department. They put all of our hair up in period peasant fashion. A man named Jon does mine. He is from England and we talk about what brought us here. A lot of the hair and make-up people are from England because they are more familiar with the time frame of the 1900's. I get a lovely little bun and my bangs hang down.

Then it's over to make-up, where we get what we fondly call "dead" make-up. We are to look as if we are in different stages of hypothermia, blue lips, dark circles, blue veins, white skin, red ears and nose. We even get our hands colored the same way. We are all ready to go by 9:00. We are told to go wait in the tent and have something to eat. The food is gross. Little did we know that this would be the norm for the rest of the film.

About 10:00, our assistant directors, Josh McLaglen and Sebastian Silva, along with Simon Crane and some stunt people come down and talk to us. They tell us of the things they will be expecting of us and the safety procedures when we enter the pool. Josh tells us that we are all equal here and that we are here for one purpose, that is to make an excellent movie. We are all human beings and we all have needs that need to be met, if we have any problems we should let them know and it will be dealt with. They tell us that there are a lot of things in the water, on the bottom and floating on top that we must be careful of. Simon introduces the people that will be watching out for us when we are in the water, so we know who to look for if we need help. They are with us for about 20 minutes and tell us it won't be much longer before we are called. Yvette, one of the production assistants, tells us if we need to use the restroom we should do it now. We do nothing, but sit around, sweat and get acquainted with each other until 4:00 p.m.

We are finally summoned to the "tank." Now the rush is on to use the restroom. We all help each other get in and out of our costumes. We realize that this will be very important when we are wet. We are all excited about finally going in and seeing all the crew and what was going on. It is kind of dark and very humid in this sound stage. On my way in I pass Billy Zane, who was there observing today. We are all quiet as we enter. There is a large stairway up to the top of the tank that also goes down into the water. We have thongs on that we leave at the bottom. Before we go up, we are to step into a large tray of water to wash our feet. We are wearing long black stockings to cover our wetsuits. We make our way into the tank, there is a man with a camera filming us as we enter. His name is Ed Marsh, he is doing the behind the scenes documentary on the film. The water feels good especially after being hot all afternoon. Josh and Sebastian are there to guide us. These men are a lot taller them me and smile as I pass.

Chairs, tables and all manner of floating debris greeted us as we entered. Under the water was worse than the top. There were pipes with big iron weights criss crossing them to hold them down. They are blowing air up around us to simulate the bubbles coming up from the sinking ship. The water has a blackish green look. We all must be very careful as we move around. I end up with my share of bruises after this day. I learned the hard way of where all this stuff is laying.

There are a lot of us that do not speak English, so after Josh talks to us again about safety and not peeing in the pool, Sebastian translates. Simon points out his people once more and tells us that after each take and the director says "cut" that an airhorn will sound so we all know that it is time to stop action. We are to stop, stand and give a thumbs up high over our heads. We are to be aware of those that are closest to us so we know that everyone is all right. If anyone is missing we are to let them know immediately. We are not to leave unless we tell the A.D.'s.

Now we are positioned and I have been placed right next to Kate Winslet who plays Rose. There are three cameras set up and a lot of lights and what would be called video village. That is where the monitors and recording equipment is. As we all watch the activities I am not sure who James Cameron is yet, but that mystery is quickly solved as the scene is almost ready to go. He takes the microphone and gives us a pep talk and what he expects to see. The scene is where the ship has just gone under and we are fighting our way to the surface. We are to be panic stricken in 28 degree water, screaming and thrashing about, trying to grab anyone or anything to save ourselves. For the next five and a half hours we begin the dying process. Mr. Cameron is right there filming it all. He keeps saying "memo", which a couple of us thinks that he is asking someone to take notes for him, but later we discover it is the name of one of the camera operators.

We get a break after about three hours. That was our first experience with the wet clothes. We all got so good at getting in and out of them. The rest of the night we did the same thing. Cameron had a camera in a big gray box to keep it dry. We all called it Moby Dick. He would take it through the groups of people for close ups of the panic that was taking place. He thanked us for our efforts that night and said he would see us Monday, same A.M. call and we were out of there. Showered off and hoped my family was waiting out front. They were and we got to bed by 11 p.m.

4

September 29, Monday

Anna and I found out we would have to be back to the set at 5:45 a.m. again. So we decided to go home and pack for a week's stay. We left the house on Sunday morning, it took us about 45 minutes to cross back into San Diego. This would prove to be the worst thing about working down here. The studio offered that bus ride back and forth to Senior Taco, but I did not want to ride those buses again if I could help it. The bus took a lot longer to get back to the border, besides that, it was cold and uncomfortable during the time we would have to be on it. Not to mention the safety factor. I bought a years worth of insurance on our Suburban and I was set.

A lot of the extras would do this every day. But we chose to stay at the house so we could get more rest. This proved to be a great benefit to us because we would be working up to 16 hours daily.

Anna and I got back down to the house on Sunday night. We had packed enough food and clothes for a week. This time we took our swimsuits to wear under our wetsuits. This way we wouldn't have to keep the wetsuits on our upper body all day. We get moved into the house and to bed by 10.

Up an at'em again at 4:30 (we really hate Mondays). It's dark out and we still don't know what the house looks like outside. We get to the studio and stop at the gate this time. We have to give them our driver's licenses and they give us our extra's I.D. tags that we are supposed to wear on our way down to the casting building. They also tell us that we are to park over in a parking lot that is pitch black and no security. I do not comply with this and park in the regular crew lot.

As we make our way down to our building we must pass by some of the construction buildings. There are a lot of Mexican men that work on the lot and this is where quite a few are working now. Obviously they do not know about sexual harassment and we have to get used to the cat calls, whistles, kissing sounds and "Hey, chica!" that we hear on a regular basis from now on. Anna was a bit uncomfortable, we laugh and hurry on our way. I asked about it later but the answer was, "we aren't in the States, you know." Well, that seemed to be the case for a lot of things, I guess. We learn to ignore them.

We get in our clothes and make-up again by 9 a.m. and are treated to a yucky breakfast again. We are all waiting in the tent and we meet another P.A. named Kari. She is teamed up with Yvette and they both tell us what to do. We learn very quickly that nothing goes according to plan. The only things that we are equal on are long hours and we all get sick. Everyone is complaining about the food and that we don't get what the crews get. A lot of these people have been there a lot longer than I have and they are not happy about that fact.

I start meeting more people from our group. Warwick, from San Diego, has a boat service there. He looks as if he could be the brother to a friend of ours in San Marcos. They were both merchant marines and both from London, but they don't even know each other. He also worked on the Queen Mary for a number of years. I then meet a couple from Seattle, Washington. James and Erica, both tall and very nice. We learn we all like old cars too. He had just bought a '65 Ford Galaxy 500 here in Mexico. He had seen my car in the lot and he really liked it. He said that he restores cars back home and that maybe if we took any of our cars to the big show up there we could get together.

4

A little before 11 a.m. we are summoned again, so we hit the bathroom on the way in. We enter from the other side of the tank today. All the cameras and lights are in different positions. Boy, the water is cold today. Find out later that over the weekend they had run out of propane to heat it with. Back to our Saturday positions and wait for further instructions. Rick and CC are close by. We all look as if we are made up for Halloween.

Kate is with us today. The girl that was in her place on Saturday was her stand in named Lori. She is dressed in a long, pastel pink and white gown. She has long red hair and stands quietly in her spot. I introduce myself and notice she is not feeling well. She has the same thing that my son Jeff has. I felt sorry for her because I knew how Jeff was feeling when I left yesterday. We talk a bit and I asked her how it felt to be nominated for the academy award for "Sense and Sensibility"? She said that it was very exciting.

Mr. Cameron arrives and reminds us of the severity of the situation that we are portraying. He tells us he liked what we did, but we needed to perfect it today. As we begin, he tells me to grab a hold of Kate and she is to twist out of my grasp. We do that a couple of times and then Cameron asks my name. I tell him, and he begins to tell me that he wants me to really grab and rough up this actress. He grabs Kate and demonstrates. I then put my hands on her shoulders and slowly try to follow his direction, but I wasn't moving fast enough and he said abruptly, "Don't pet her!" I responded timidly that I was just getting a feel of what he wanted. He then said for me to grab at her face and to let him see my nails. They were too long and he didn't want Kate to get scratched. He asked for a stunt woman to be brought in. I said I would bite my nails off. He sort of smiled as he turned back to the camera. I just could not get what he wanted fast enough and there wasn't time for a lot of practice. I could have done this to someone I know, but to mug the actress that I just met was abit overwhelming. I stepped back and let the stunt woman take my place for the next couple of takes. Boy was I disappointed.

On to the next scene with a group of three stuntmen that Cameron was working on now. They were to fight over a barrel to try to stay afloat. It was very realistic and violent. Cameron stops and wants to put blood on a couple of the guys. He walks past me and we watch him apply this pasty stuff and then squirt on the runny blood. I wondered if we would get any and commented to CC because she was closer. As Cameron came back I turn to her again and said "I guess we don't get any." Cameron asked what I said and I just told him I guess we don't get any blood. He looked down at me and said "You spoke to soon, come here." I stepped up and he put a nice juicy gash on my forehead over my right eye and down to my temple, and then put on the runny blood. I was the only woman that got blood. There after I was dubbed his "bloody dead chick." He also starts calling me by name and so does Sebastian and Josh. I get some teasing from my friends about it, but it's all in fun.

As the day wears on we are getting colder. I could tell that it was really getting to Kate and I felt sorry for her, because she had been in a lot longer than we had. When we got our break the crew stayed in and apparently kept working. The food is yucky again. The showers are cold, there is nothing and nowhere to get warm, this will prove to be the longest and one of the most miserable days I will experience. All the other days we have been down here the sun has been out and the temperature in the 80's, but not today. It is overcast and cold, what we call "June gloom" in San Diego.

Back in we go, Josh asks how I'm doing, I just say "Fine, but cold," he said that it would be taken care of by tomorrow. In our same spots again, back to one or otra vez as Sebastian says. The stuntmen are still fighting over the barrel just behind Kate and me. The cameras, Cameron and crew members are in front of us. We have been instructed to get under the water if we can. Kate holds on to a couple of weight bags so she can go all the way down for a 5 count, others for 7 to 10. As we begin another shot, Kate goes under and Cameron yells "Action." At that moment an air hose breaks loose and flies up out of the water with a terrible noise and hits Gary in the face. Kate is still under the water next to me. I reach for Kate to pull her up out of the way, but the people in the crew concerned about Gary lunge forward. It all happened so fast, they forgot that Kate was still under water and she gets stepped on. This is a bad thing happening here. Cameron is pissed and wants to know what happened. Kate is crying, Gary bleeding, Cameron mad and we just watch. Kate goes out for a while, Gary goes to get the side of his nose stitched up and Cameron gets Moby Dick to go through the crowd again. We get out at 10 p.m. and go home, take a hot shower and collapse.

5

October 1, Tuesday

Up at the same time again. Anna and I pray it is warm today. We are starting to be recognized at the gate now and just wave as we go in. The parking lot is still dark and we won't go out there. I tell them that if they want us out there that we need lights and a guard, because we are already hearing about people's cars getting broke into in the unfenced area. As we pass by the sound stage we see jacuzzis waiting for us and we find the showers warm! Apparently a lot of people bit the dust yesterday and won't be back. Amy rattled some cages and got us the spas.

Trish is really getting sick. Ellen and her get cold really fast because they are so thin. CC isn't doing so well either. Yesterday took its toll, I hear from people all day about how they aren't feeling well. A lot of ear aches, and upper respiratory infections would develop over the next week or so. I have noticed that I am starting to lose my voice a little, because of the screaming I have been doing, but hey, Mr. C likes it and has told me so.

Living the Legend: The Journal of a Titanic Background Actress

I meet a young man from England today. His name is Julian and he is Simon Crane's brother-in-law. He is tall, nice and very funny. I like to listen to his story about his big vacation that ends with how he gets on the film and how Simon wants to kill him, love his accent. I also meet Barbara, who lives in Rosarito. Ellen and Barbara have become some of our floating dead people. When we go into our thrashing routine we must be very careful of them. They are virtually at our mercy because they can not see what is going on or who is coming at them. The first few shots were bad in that respect and Josh had to really lay into some people for not watching what they were doing. Barbara was climbed on and pushed under, so were some others.

They have removed some of the air pipes, so moving around is not as perilous. We meet George (we call him gorgeous because of his body) he takes care of the underwater stuff and watches everyone during the takes. Laurie Crane, Simon's cousin, takes care of the water safety and watching us too. He was working on the deep-sea oil rigs before coming out here. He's another really nice, tall Englishman.

Now we are set to go again. We are doing more of the same. Thank God the water is warm again. Mr. Cameron wants to speak to us and tell us what to do. I see someone hand him a microphone. He fusses with it a bit and all of a sudden the mic is flying through the air in my direction. It splashes down about 3 feet from me. I guess it wasn't working right. I see George recover it later. Leonardo is with us today, he plays Jack. Anna is jealous because I get to be close to him today, but I don't get to meet him as I did Kate. Josh has me floating dead behind them and my back is turned, so I can't do what I did before with Kate. During this scene a little black French Bulldog is used. He is adorable, has great big eyes and is about 10 in. tall. Cameron tells everyone not to hurt "his" little dog. The dog is to swim out of nowhere and lead Kate and Leo to a large piece of wreckage. We only do this shot about seven times because the dog is becoming tired, even though a diver is holding the dog from underneath! During this time I just lay motionless in the water. John "JB" Buckley, head of lighting, has to stand directly in front of me to hold a light that is needed for the shot. We get to visit about ourselves in between takes. Now we break for lunch.

There are catering tents outside. One for the crew and one for us. We can easily go into the crew's tent and they have great stuff in there. Well, we are quickly told that we can't have their stuff. We have to have the slop in the "extras" area. Too much Mexican candy and not enough choices. Nothing but coffee and you have to beg for tea. While I was waiting outside near the tent, Jon Landau, the producer sees me standing there and comes up to me and tells me that he is so proud of all of us for the job we are doing in the water. I thanked him and as he was leaving, he asked me to pass his sentiment along. The jacuzzis are great and we can't thank Amy enough for them. The food still sucks and someone has gotten a suggestion sheet together for all of us to sign. We will see if this helps.

Back in we go, after waiting for quite sometime. I get to meet the lady that takes care of Kate's wardrobe. Her name is Marsha, she has thick, long red hair and is just as tall as I am, five feet to be exact, she is very nice and talks to me a lot when we are waiting around. Cameron is filming other scenes that involved Kate and Leo on that wreckage. We don't get to see a lot of that. They are having trouble with the piece that Kate is supposed to climb onto. They pull it out of the water and Cameron starts to fix it himself. It must have been right, because they didn't fuss with it again. We are only in for 7 or 8 hours today, but we are still there 16 hours total. We are home by 10:30, collapse, but still end up talking about the Bible for two hours before we finally fall asleep.

6

October 2, Wednesday

We don't have to be on set until 7a.m.! It is almost light outside when we get there. We are told when we got to the gate that the parking lot they want us to use has lighting now. I thanked them and we went out to the new lot.

We find some changes in our catering. We hope that this is a positive sign and again thank those in charge…a lot. There are changes in our make-up also. Little did we know what we were in for. I am to be "frozen," wax is melted and applied to my hair, eyebrows and lashes. They apply it with paint brushes and Q-Tips. Before they put the wax on my hair they rub a little bit of Vaseline through it, this is to make it so the wax doesn't stick so bad, they should have used Pam. Now we get very dead make-up, like what we had before, but more intense. Medical adhesive is applied on various areas of our face and hands, then they apply this stuff that looks like gelatin. It swells when they spray it with water, but it stays whitish and looks like ice. We are guinea pigs at this point, because they have never used this before. We also are told that it is very expensive, about $25 for three or four ounces. They soon discover that the two layers that they have applied are too much, they only need one application. This stuff dries out and contracts, so through out the day we keep getting sprayed with water to keep is puffy and soft. When this happens it expands, so our face feels as if it is having contractions all day. When it dries it feels like big crusty scabs, when wet it feels like snot. Some of the guys keep pulling it off and this makes the make-up people upset. I just leave it alone.

Mr. Cameron takes special joy in making fun of some of us. It is refreshing when such a busy man will stop in the middle of everything, look down at me and laugh at what I look like. He said "You have an ice mustache, notice I didn't say nice," I smile as he walked away and he added "I really like the effect though." He also told Rick that he looked like a walrus.

Today would be different, much more emotional then before. Maybe because we are not moving around and I have time to imagine the past we are portraying. All the pipes and hoses have been removed, a lifeboat is now in the debris field. The lights are low and it is quiet as we enter the water. It's almost as if the crew had a sort of reverence about what was going to be filmed today. It is all a little eerie. Sebastian and Josh tell us where to stand. Everyone is to be dead now. The lifeboat is coming back to search for survivors. We are told what to expect and how to maintain our positions without floating to far away from them. We are also told that they are very happy with a lot of the footage already shot. That even Kate was disturbed at some of the footage because it appeared to be so real.

Now we are ready, Josh, as usual does his all familiar and ever present "SHHH! SHH! SHH!" then "background action," except this time instead of saying "bring it life," he quietly adds "dead, dead, dead." We all thought that to be one of the funnier commands that we had heard so far. As the shot begins the lifeboat rows slowly into the debris field. We hear Officer Lowe (Ioan Gruffudd), crying, "Is there anyone out there, OH GOD, is there anyone alive?" Laurie is holding a light as he leans over the bow, he replies, in the same distressing tone, "They're dead Sir, they're all dead!" The lifeboat rows through slowly, moving some of us with the oars. We trust James, Greg and the others, not to hit us in the head as they pass. Although, they do have fun dripping water on our faces to see us flinch. I can hear the boat approach, I am in a position to open one eye and see what is coming. Greg's oar comes up out of the water, over my head and down under my butt. For him to make another stroke on que, he has to lift me a bit, so to help him I just kind of push off the bottom and turn slowly out of the way. Later we laugh about it, because I told him to be kind to me with that ore. Also, I find out that he has two other brothers on the set, Geoff and George. They have a business in Oceanside, only about 15 minutes from our house. Well, we do a few more takes and we sit around while they shoot the scenes of rescuing Kate and a Chinese man (Van Ling). Here again we can not see a lot of what is happening. I know that Kate is on what looks to be a very elaborately carved door. This is the same piece that I saw them fix the other day. She is blowing a whistle that was either taken from a dead man or given to her before her and Leo are separated. She is very weak, close to being unconscious from hypothermia. The only way she is making any noise with the whistle is with the rhythm of her breathing. We wrap and go to make-up for them to remove all the stuff in our hair and on our face, it took over an hour and it was not pleasant.

We don't get home until 10:30 again. Before we go to bed Anna and I tell each other how we felt when Officer Lowe would speak. We both agreed that it really got to us. By the third take of hearing "is there anyone alive out there?" I found myself sobbing as heard those words over and over today. Now alone with the lights out, I think back on those words again, it takes me to the time when it was real, I can't help but cry myself to sleep.

7

October 3, Thursday

Don't have to be in until 7 a.m. again. My mind still filled with last night and I wonder what is in store for us today. I get frozen again and must make sure that I have my bloody gash, it really looks cool with ice in it. Five others get frozen too. Anna doesn't work, she is to be in a lifeboat and can't be with us dead folk. She sits contented and watches the freezing process.

The six of us are special, we are to wait until Cameron needs us for some close shots. Well, we wait and wait. All day we sit around, eat and talk, but we never get called. We get to sit around and watch everyone else be tortured. That fake ice on our faces is really uncomfortable and itchy when it gets totally dry. At least we can watch the activity awhile. We can see the Chinese man get rescued. The light that Laurie is using is a reproduction of the real thing. It is an oblong wooden box about 14 in. long, with a battery inside. It has a glass globe on the end that swivels up and down. For what it is, it casts a fairly wide beam. The men in the boat can hear a faint call in the darkness. As they search frantically for the right direction, the Chinese man can see the light moving back and forth and musters all his strength to cry out even louder. The lifeboat finally spots the man, who is trying to stand on debris and wave, but each time he almost falls. They pull him in as they draw along side. As he falls into the boat he is covered with blankets and reassured he is now safe. I think again what this really must have been like and what it will look like on film.

We are now on a break. Once again we are told to stay out of the crew tent. So friends we have made with the crew bring us some good stuff. The food at lunch did improve a little today, but the snack table still sucks out loud. I become acquainted with more of my fellow extras. Wade is a Chuck Norris look alike that has come down from San Diego. I also get to know Maria and Jill, they are here with their children. Their families live locally. When lunch is over we all sit around the spa area waiting for the call to go in. Some go, some stay, I end up with the ones that stay. Finally, they call us in, but we stand inside for a while then we are told to go back outside. We wrap at 9:30. Not wanting to sit for an hour to get "thawed," I decide to go home in full make-up and thus conduct another experiment for the hair and make-up departments. You should have seen the looks I got at the gate when I left. When I get to the house, I shower, but didn't wash my face. I laid a towel on my pillow and didn't move all night. My face was stuck to the towel when I woke up. I just peeled it off and I was ready to go.

8

October 4, Friday

Up at 6 a.m. Anna and I are really sick of bananas, we thought we would be smart and bring some with us when we came back to the house for our stay down here, but that has been the only fresh fruit to grab on set, now the fridge at the house reeks of them. They do have sliced watermelon and mango, but when they set it out this morning it had been frozen from the day before. That kind of stuff just doesn't work frozen. They just don't get it.

Anna decides to ask if she can work today, because more people have not come back. So they let her and put her in the deep background. Make-up and hair treat me as a novelty, they lead me around the shop and show me to everyone. They are amazed that all my make-up stayed on this long. All that is needed is a little touch up on the face and redo my hands and I am ready to go again. We wait around until about 1 p.m. We are then summoned to what we are now calling the "cement pond."

Living the Legend: The Journal of a Titanic Background Actress

The lifeboat is now on the other side. We are placed in its path so that one of the sailors can reach down and pick us up by the life vest and present us to the camera on board. I meet Linda Kern, who plays a prominent 3rd Classer and Steve Wehmeyer, leader of the Celtic band, Gaelic Storm, in steerage. They are "dead" with me. I was first to be picked up by the lifeboat, but then Josh moved me next to Linda. They put crystal gray contacts in her eyes so she could be open eyed dead. She really looks freaky and does some monster impressions in between takes. Because we actually float, we tend to move off our marks. After each take I help her back to her mark because all she can see is blurry movement and light. I talk to Steve and he tells me of how his band was picked for the film. They were at a Renaissance Fair and some scouts for the film were there looking for a band. Theirs was the first to be asked to send in a sound track. As production proceeds it's going to get more exciting. After a time, we are told to rotate around to opposite positions. They are ready to do Ellen's much anticipated "dead frozen mommy" scene. We knew that she would be doing this and had kidded her about having to hold a baby, too. We had no idea that she actually would. Cameron positioned her and applied the make-up he wanted on her himself. That took about 20 minutes. It is to be one of the "tear your heart out" scenes, as they described it. We are all quiet as Cameron works. But, every once in awhile people start talking too loud and Josh says "quiet please" and Sebastian will add "What part of 'quiet please' do you not understand? Quiet or Please?!" We shoot this for some time and the lifeboat continues to our end of the pool. I get picked up once more but I doubt it will be used. We wrap about 11 p.m. and we tell Ellen that she did a great job. She had been in that position for quite sometime and said her neck got a little stiff. On our way out to the car, Anna and I take some pictures next to a lifeboat and we also meet Zubie. He is the construction safety supervisor and takes some time to fill us in on how big the outside tank is and how it all works. To bed by midnight, tomorrow we go home.

9

October 5, Saturday

We are up and loaded to go by 10 a.m. We head home and can't wait to stop and eat at Mickey D's. Never thought I would be glad to see this kind of junk food. God bless America. We love it! Back home by noon and just sleep.

I have no work for five days. It's a good thing, because I have started an ear infection and have almost lost my voice. I'm able to rest and reflect on the past week. I tell my family all that has happened and all the people that I have met. I'm amazed at the progress on the ship. The funnels on Titanic were all uneven and they have gotten those all at the right level now. More work on the upper deck is finished, but it still is not as tall as it should be. It is harder to go around and look at things. They don't like us to wander around the sets anymore.

I think about all the things that Josh and Sebastian have told us to do like; Background-ACTION! BRING IT ALIVE!!!. Everybody down and get wet! Lunch, one half. On your marks. Otra vez or back to one. SILENCEO, POR FAVOR!!! Pictures up. THUMBS UP!!! Rolling, and

AAACTION!!! But the one that haunts us all is Josh's SHHH! SHH! SHH! This man is unbelievable. I have never seen anyone chew gum or smoke cigarettes as fast as he does. I later find out that he is Victor McLaglen's grandson. He is the man that fought with John Wayne in the "Quiet Man," and appeared in many other John Wayne films.

By the third day at home I start getting antsy, I give the set a call and ask what is going on. They are shooting 1st Class scenes and will call me when 3rd Class is ready to go again.

10

October 10, Friday

I am back down to the set at 9 a.m. We are going to be dry today. We will be inside the common room for 3rd Class. This is the inside set that I have seen under construction next door to our cement pond. It is an exact duplicate to the photos that I have seen of the ship. All white and clean, with wooden benches, some tables and the swivel chairs that remind you of captain's chairs. There is a piano in one corner that will be accompanied by the band later on.

I have the same outfit that they originally fitted me with, but they never washed the blouse. It stinks sooo bad, even Ellen starts sneezing around me. I tell the ladies in wardrobe and they said they would take care of it. Time goes by and we are almost ready to go inside. I still haven't gotten a new shirt. I start to have a reaction to the mildew and I start itching, under my arms, my back, chest and neck. I finally go and take it off. I go and find Amy Arnold, from wardrobe, she is really busy but she knows I am getting upset and having problems with skin irritation. I have to go out to the tent and listen to instructions that our leaders are giving us. Just before we are finished, Amy brings me a couple of shirts to try on. I have to do it right in the tent because we are starting to go to the set. Some of the ladies stand around me and Amy helps. As I remove my T-shirt she sees that I have broken out all over my upper body. She asks if I will be all right and I said yes and thanked her very much for her concern and help.

At the time, we think it's great that we will be on a dry set for a change. Especially those that have been sick and developed weird little skin rashes from being in wetsuits that many hours a day. I'm glad I won't be screaming anymore for a while. Little did we know that this would be the worst set that we would be on, at least for some of us.

As we enter, it is hot, very hot, smoky and stuffy. At first there is some air conditioning. Josh greets me and tells us to go to the back side of the room for instructions. He marries some of us off. Ellen and I stay single, but she has a baby. We call this her "ugly baby" and it will be with her for quite sometime. We are to act as if we are in our living room, so to speak, casual and visiting with family and friends, moving about and watching all that is going on. We are to be excited, for we are on our way to a new world and new life. Children are playing and exploring the surroundings. Cameron paints a vivid picture. Groups of men drinking beer and playing checkers. Women knitting and taking care of children. Lots of smoking…real smoking. We are told if you got'em, smoke'em!!! The prop people keep the cigarettes coming. They have to cut the filters off so they look authentic. Some men have pipes and cigars. The bawdy women smoke in public. Just about everyone smokes, except Cameron. The set is miserable, it must be 95 degrees or more. It doesn't take long for us to wish we were back in the water again.

We are to provide the atmosphere for Kate and Leo (Rose and Jack) to meet. As she comes down the staircase, she momentarily disrupts the activities going on. It is not usual for 1st Class to mingle with 3rd. I am standing near a bench when action starts, I move around greeting people and find interest in watching two older men (Pete and John, (70 years old or so) play checkers, I ask them how they are doing and they respond to me with jokes and laughter. None of which will be heard, I might add. We do this over and over. I start worrying about Pete. He has on some heavy clothes and is really sweating. We have to beg for water, later some people get heat stroke. It is the worst day since the tank got cold. They were either freezing or frying us. I got to a point that I was really feeling sick and had to move over to what little air I could find. Sebastian knew that I was not where I should be and called out for me. I was just behind him, but out of sight. He asked me if I was OK and I said that I really needed to cool off because I was so hot. As he put his hand on my shoulder he said "Yeah, you are, just remember where you stand." I nod and say "ok". Not a problem, if I had learned anything by now it is where I'm supposed to stand.

Mr. Cameron moved the camera around to different locations in the room. At one point he puts the camera just opposite me as I stood at the table. He has me move to the side so he has a good shot up to the staircase as Kate comes down. He has my belly in the shot as well. He asked me what I did as I stood at the table, so I showed him. I was talking to the men that were playing checkers and as I spoke I moved my hand. Cameron told me to do this during one take. I guess I did it to much or it looked like I was conducting a symphony and he stops and tells me "Stop it, you're driving me crazy! Just stand there!" But I didn't take it personally. We were all hot and tired. It just didn't look right being so close to the camera.

The catering is back to bad again. This is everyone's pet peeve. When we come back from lunch everything is turned around. Some people have been wrapped for the day, but the group of us that were near the camera last keep going. Jimmy, who runs the steadycam, has been in working with us all afternoon. This is a very interesting piece of equipment. He has a harness with weights that counter that of the camera. It gives the operator great control and very smooth movement even if he runs. It is fascinating to watch him work and move around the way he does.

We roll until 11:30 p.m. Cameron thanks us as we leave, and says "See ya tomorrow." I have to drive home tonight. My son, Jeff got a call to come down for a fitting tomorrow afternoon, he's so excited.

11

October 11, Saturday

It is 2 a.m. and I just get home. I'm having trouble with my truck, and won't be able to make the 8 a.m. set call. I go in and call the set to inform them of my problem, they tell me to call back at 7 a.m. So I do and get the answering machine. I said I would be in ASAP, that I was doing the best I could. So we do a temporary fix and get to the set by 2 p.m. No one had gotten my message yet. I am sure glad that I knew the name of the person I talked to last night.

Jeff's fitting appointment is at 2:30 and he still sits around and waits. He is finally taken back to the fitting area. He emerges as a 3rd Class passenger, just like me! His outfit looks good, too. He has a hat, vest and jacket with tweed pants. He is not fitted with a wetsuit because he is not able to endure the long hours. He also has too much school to keep up with. So he can't make any long term commitments to the film.

I get in my water clothes again. We were so glad we didn't have to be on the dry set, at least for a while. While we are waiting around, I get a chance to introduce Jeff to some of my new friends. Ralph takes a real liking to Jeff and shows him around that night.

We get called to the tank at about 5 p.m. We are doing a scene with Billy Zane tonight. Some of the men that are sailors have been in for most of the afternoon. They came out a couple of times for a break and they looked tired. Some of them are wearing thick wool clothing and you could tell they were hot. Dinner time…joy! Those of us that had not been working yet, let those that had been, go first in line for another fine meal.

As we enter the cement pond we see Billy standing in a collapsible boat. He is holding a little girl in his arms. We wait off to the side for a couple of takes and just watch until we are needed. Sebastian has his airhorn, which he doesn't use at first. As action starts we see six guys under one side of the boat. They push up on that side of it to give the effect of a wave hitting it. The little girl is fine until the next take when Sebastian has to use the horn. Billy and the others in the boat are fighting off those that are trying to climb in. It is loud, people screaming, and Billy is using an oar to hit people with. That didn't bother the girl at all, but when the take was over and that horn went off it scared her to death and she just could not stop crying. After numerous attempts to calm her, Cameron said that was enough and stopped trying to shoot that scene.

Now it was our turn. This time it would be a lot rougher. We are to rush the boat as the first funnel falls from the forward deck of the ship. This is what causes the wave that the six guys are duplicating. It is really funny the way this is being done, half of the set is surrounded with green screen, from top to bottom. Cameron tells us what we are to do. He has a flashlight that he has directed at the screen. We are to act as if we are hearing a loud metal crunching sound as we are swimming away from the ship. When we hear this noise we turn for a moment to see what it is. Cameron then moves the light in a sweeping motion down the screen and yells "funnel, funnel, funnel!" We then panic as we see the funnel crashing down on us. Those that are near the boat try to climb in. Action begins and I am near the boat, but I can't get in because I die. So Josh tells me to just fight the best I can and not climb in. Wade is next to me and he makes it in. As I get to the boat I see stuntman Gary reaching for me. I am thinking to myself, I wonder what he's going to do to me. Now the camera is on my left so I can't go that way. I have to go to Gary. He reaches down for me after he helps Wade in. Wade then turns to help me. Gary grabs me by the back of my lifevest and Wade grabs my right arm. Gary starts poking me in my right side (that is away from camera view) and tells me "don't laugh, don't laugh." Wade is no help, because all he can do is laugh. I know now why I die, they kill me!

Happy with just 3 or 4 shots, Cameron has us get out and take a break and has the boats changed. Lifeboat 2 is brought in. Sebastian tells me to get in the boat and to just cover up my head so no one can see me. Simon is in charge and we are rowing away from the rear of the ship as the propellers are coming up out of the water. We must get away quickly. Simon is yelling, "Row, row for your lives!" Most of us are reacting in fear. As we face the green screen, they have put a row of pink X's for us to have a focus point. Later we see the monitors that have the propellers in the picture and it makes it a little easier to imagine what we are doing. This scene is later used in the trailer for the film. After just 4 or 5 takes of this we wrap at 10:30 p.m.

Just as Jeff and I are getting ready to leave, we are offered a hotel room. We gratefully decline because we have the house. As we get to the house we see that there are people there! It is mid-night and we don't know who is there. We hurry back to the set and we catch Maggie as she is leaving. She tells us to go the Don Luis in Rosarito. I have never been there and it seems as if it takes forever to find it. It looks like a pit and we are wondering what in the world are we getting into. Further inspection reveals that it is like a little oasis in the parking lot, very nice and clean. We get separate rooms and a good night's sleep.

12

October 12, Saturday

Back to the studio at 8 a.m. Some of our fearless leaders have gotten sick. With all the hours they have put in it's no wonder. There seems to be a different air around today. Can't figure out what it is, but there is definitely something wrong. They are shooting on 2 sets today, maybe it is just stress I sense. I later find out that there has been some very important paperwork lost and some heads are rolling.

Cameron is shooting the gym scene today. This is the one I originally was going to do. I am glad that things worked out like this because I would have only had 3 or 4 days of work. Sebastian is in charge of us today. He greets me as I enter and tells me to do what I was doing last night. It is 11 a.m. so we are getting started early today. We have our wetsuits on, but don't get wet. I have mine pulled down so I don't get hot. Roman and Magda, our very active and lovable elderly couple, are with us today as well. They have their wetsuits on too, but leave them pulled up under their clothes. They start to worry some of us because we can see that they are getting hot. When we take a break we talk them into taking the suits down off their upper body. We are just filming more of what we did last night, but at different angles. They bring us trays of goodies today. Really good taquitos, we feel special. It is a lot different working with Sebastian. Some feel as if they can get away with more, although he does keep us animals under control. We respect him greatly, and have fun.

Out for lunch about 4 p.m. we kick back and just visit. I get a hassle from someone in the office for having Jeff with me. This really upsets me because they know my situation. I am 4 hours round trip from the set and could not take him home last night. I have been there and done everything I've been asked to do. I asked them to please cut me a little slack on this matter, it wasn't as if I did it all the time and the house that I was staying in was not available this weekend, or else he would have stayed there. He had nowhere to go. So with that they left it alone. None of us could believe that was happening or that they gave me grief for letting Jeff eat with us that day. Nothing else better to do I guess, so they hassle one of their good people to see if they will take it. It was ridiculous.

About 5:30 we are moved back up to the jacuzzi area. Some stay out, some go in for tank duty. I stay out because they are shooting close up shots that I can't be in this time. Jeff brought his guitar and entertains us a little. There are a couple of other guys that can play too and Jeff lets them use his guitar to play for us as well. It is enjoyable and interesting since they all had different styles.

I get called in about 8 p.m. We are to be a group of swimmers that are trying to get away from the rear of the ship. We are all getting slap happy, everything seems to make us laugh and Wade starts making fart sounds in between takes. I can't stop laughing. During one shot one of our group thinks it's over and stands up in the middle of the take with thumbs up, but we aren't done. Sebastian thought something might be wrong but quickly realizes all is well and this guy is hearing things. Everyone is laughing by now, especially Sebastian. We finally do get the job done and wrap about 9:30.

On the way out we stop and look at the 5 million gallon indoor set where the Grand Staircase and dining room are under construction. We see that there are 3 levels of the interior of the ship. All of this will be sunk in the tank that holds it. Can't wait to see that.

    I take Jeff home that night. It took at least 2 hours to cross the border that night. While we were waiting in line we saw a guy run past our truck and to a car several feet in front of us. He had a stick and broke the window of the car and started beating on the drive. There was nothing we could do except watch and hope that it would stop. We could see the police come running from the check point to help and the guy ran off, we don't know if he ever got caught. The driver that was assaulted refused treatment and that was that…crazy. We get home by 2 a.m. I have another few days off to rest.

13

October 22, Tuesday

I get a call to come down for Wednesday. Anna is already down there. I go over to her house and get her things for the week's stay and go down that night. I get to the set at 7:30 p.m. I am excited because they are shooting in the interior of the ship. I have been asked to work if needed, but I don't have to be dressed until that time. This makes it easy for me to stay and watch the filming that night.

We are all sitting down stairs in the dining room. I walk around a little and look at everything. It's fun to make fun of everyone in costume and to look "normal" to everyone else. Anna is in her cashier's outfit, but it looks more like a nurse's uniform. She also has on very pale make-up. We have to stay in the sitting room area just forward of the dining room. Unbelievable is the only way to describe it. The walls and ceilings are all white with intricate carving and designs. The carpet is greenish with a reddish floral design. Wicker furniture in the sitting area, green leather and wooden chairs are in the dining room. The tables are set formal style, two plates, three forks, two knives and napkins folded on the plates. Each table has flowers and a silver lamp with a white shade. In the center of the room at each end, are large buffets lavishly adorned with flowers and food on silver trays. All of the wood appears to be oak, after close inspection, I discover that a lot of it is. There are windows that line each side. At first I think they are plastic, but discover with amazement that they are real leaded glass windows. The carpeting in this room is more decorative, but the same colors as in the sitting room. I later find out that these carpets are reproductions of the real thing that were on the real ship and manufactured by the same company. The attention to detail is phenomenal. Although it is sickening to think that it will all be destroyed in the coming flood scenes.

After looking around, we just sit and visit with each other. We can't see any of the filming because they are up above us. We can only hear some of the activity. We wrap at mid-night.

14

October 23, Wednesday

Up at 9 a.m. and to the set at 10:45. We sit and wait for our call. That is all we do, all day long, sit and wait. At least we are able to find comfortable areas to wait in. We talk, play games, pace and try to sleep. Anna does get called in for a couple shots. Josh hurries through as scenes are being changed and says "hello" to a few of us. Jon Landau also comes by with a quick greeting. We can tell things are going slow and to stay put. Sebastian makes an appearance about 8 p.m. and wraps a lot of us. I tell him that I have to stay around and wait for Anna because I have the car, so he checks if she is really needed. Apparently not and she is wrapped too. To bed at 11 p.m.

October 24, Thursday. To the set at 10 a.m. breakfast, disgusting as usual. We find out, to our great displeasure, that we are in the common room, and it's hot, hot, hot again. We have to beg for water and air. We did not finish in here before because Danny Nucci's wife was expecting and it was their first baby. We hear that it was written in his contract to leave when she delivered the baby. Good planning! Now he has returned and we are ready to continue with more dancing and brawling. Later, I get to speak to him and he is very happy to share the news about his new little girl. He really is a nice guy, but he smokes these awful smelling cigars all the time.

On one scene, some of the guys are standing near Kate. One guy is supposed to run into the other and that guy spills his drink all over Kate. Wade and Hans get the honors. Josh kneels behind Wade so he can "que" him. Something happens, Hans hits Wade and Wade spills the drink on Kate. All this is done without Josh giving the signal. If the camera had been rolling it might have looked great, but Josh gets upset and they have to clean Kate up and start over again. This was shot about six times. Because we are so uncomfortable the time between shots seems to take forever. They keep smoking the set with fake smoke, at least it's not as bad as the real thing was when they did it before.

Now they are concentrating on Kate. They are trying to make it look as if she stands on her tip toes, then losses her balance and falls into Leo's arms. Falling into Leo is easy, now they want to show her feet. They try a number of things. One way of doing this it to put a balance bar in front of her so she can lift herself up, but the most amusing try is when they drop a couple of cables from above to hook to a belt around her waist and pull her up. After trying that for at least an hour or more, they decide that getting a professional dancer to do it will be better.

As the day slowly wears on, some fall victim to the heat. I hear of someone fainting and a couple of others hugging the porcelain god. We keep telling ourselves that "they" (the crew) are suffering, too. When we get breaks the crew usually stays in and works.

We finally break for dinner. I only have some tomatoes, that's all that is really edible, besides it's just good to be outside. Ellen and I tell Anna about what we are doing inside, because she is not working tonight. The casting office has let her help with phone calls and miscellaneous. things.

When we entered today, Ellen and I were seated on one of the long benches in the center of the room. We were placed about 15 feet behind Kate. We are to be visiting and milling around talking to people, occasionally glancing at what Kate and Leo are doing. Ellen has her baby with her and talks with other mothers in the room. Some of the dance scenes are also being done, but without the band. Because I am not main core, all I can do is stand on the sidelines. With some others, we make our own dance area that is secondary to the main group. Cameron has instructed Josh to tell us to act naturally to the circumstances and action around us. They must like it because we keep doing it. During one shot, one of the dance group loses it and gets mad. She starts yelling at Sebastian about the heat and not having any water like the crew has access to. After that, the effort is made to make sure we do get water.

Now it's time to go back in and it's like pulling teeth to go back into the sweat box. We linger back as long as possible. Greeted again by Mr. Cameron. That simple "Hello" goes along way for us. He addresses us all and tells us we must keep in mind what we are doing here. (We kid each other saying, "When I find out what it is I'll let you know"). He knows we are hot and tired. We continue on with more of the same and finish with what he is looking for. Wrap at 11p.m. Don't get to sleep until 3 a.m. because Anna won't stop talking. I asked her what they did to her in the office to make her so hyper. We head for home on Friday morning. I get a call to come back on Monday.

15

October 28, Monday

I get to the studio at 7:30 and we are on the set by 11. It is still hot, but they do have the air conditioning in a couple more places. More dancing, but this time we watch Kate and Leo up on the cargo hold cover. Jimmy has the steady-cam and he is Kate's partner as they spin around. This gives the effect of the two looking at each other during the dancing. It is not as easy as it looks and takes time in setting it up to look right. Measurements are constantly being checked along with the angles and lighting. The finished product gives us an even flow of movement. We become acquainted with four of the dance company. A nice group of kids that are very talented. One guy is really tall and he does the high kicks and stuff like that. During one shot he tears the seat out of his pants. We find out that the choreographer (Lynne Hockney) worked with Arnold Schwarzenegger on *True Lies*, she taught him to tango. As all this is going on, we clap, laugh and do our own little jigs.

Now the camera angles change. Kate and Leo jump down off the hatch cover and move around the floor. As they are dancing, Josh calls me over to him. He tells me to enter the crowd and make my way through moving past the camera. He wants to create a lot of movement around the room. So we have a circular motion and a figure 8 happening all at once. The band is playing and the atmosphere is happy and carefree. At one point, Cameron is filming the band and all the players. They really are good and it is fun interacting with them.

It's break time and we can't wait to get outside again. Food is well… crappy again. We meet some people that are here for the first time today. There are two that are really a pain in the ass. They go where they shouldn't go during the shots and put themselves in scenes that they weren't in before. We told them that they shouldn't be doing that, but they ignore us. By the end of the night, one trouble maker vows to never return and to cause trouble for the film. He is never seen around the set again, he changes his clothes and leaves the studio.

It's time to go back in and we continue on with the same things. The camera angles are the only things that are different. Amy came in to talk to Sebastian about what will be happening tomorrow. They are supposed to start the night shooting on the poop-deck soon. Amy called me over to them and tells me that I probably won't be able to do that shoot, something about not enough harnesses to go around. I am crushed, I really wanted to do it, but what could I say? I just said OK and turned to walk away. They both could see how disappointed I was, actually on the verge of tears. Amy calls me back and said they would see what they could do. The rest of the night was hard to get through, because I couldn't stop thinking about not being on the poop-deck. I had really been looking forward it. We have been watching it get built, seen it being tested and talking about being up there for a month now. When asked about wanting to be on it, I jumped at the chance and expressed my interest early on. The testing that we did at the swimming pool rated us at 1-10. I pulled a 9 at swimming and a 10 with everything else. I had done everything asked of me and I wanted to be part of the next phase. I managed to get through the night. Glad to wrap at 1 a.m. I really feel tired, but muster enough strength to have some fun with the band. They start beating the drum to the beat of "We Will Rock You". I, being the ham that I am, start clapping and singing the words. Others join in and we rock the Common Room as the camera crew, A.D.'s and even Mr.

Cameron look on. I wish I could have seen a video of that sight. 1912 3rd Classers, rockin' out to 1990's music. Even after being there all day, we stuck around in that awful hot room to top off the night and send everyone out smiling. This will be one moment that all that are present will remember. Just before I left, Amy tells me to come in tomorrow, that I could at least be up with the first group that didn't need harnesses. I am excited now and all my friends feel better too. Ellen and I take a room at the Don Luis. To bed at 2 a.m. Tomorrow we get to the stern!

16

October 29, Tuesday

At the studio at 8:15. We have a new leader join the team. Her name is Bo Bobak. She is from North Carolina and worked on *The Last of the Mohicans, The Fugitive,* and *A Time to Kill,* just to name a few. She seems very personable and is very easy to communicate with. We hit it off right away.

Turns out that I do get a harness. Last night Amy and Sebastian said they would see what they could do and here I am! I can't thank them enough. This is great, nice sunny day, crystal clear. We can see all the way up and down the coast. As we assemble to go to the set, I feel giddy inside, like a little kid getting on my first rollercoaster ride. As we approach, we can't believe how big it is. At least 150 feet long, this 90% scale model of the stern rests on a giant "I" beam structure. There are four huge hinges that are not as big as I thought but, are at least 4 x 5 feet, these allow the structure to move. The giant hydraulics that lift and lower the structure can be seen as well. We don't get to inspect things to closely, because we are hurrying to get up on deck. Simon Crane is with us today because he is responsible for the stunt coordination and our safety. Everyone else is shooting on an interior set. Simon tells us what to do, to be quiet and listen. He is very positive about the rules, if you screw around, you're off. He will not tolerate messing around, because he is responsible for our lives. He tells us to find a spot on the rail and to put our safety cables around it. His stunt crew comes around to make sure we are properly secured. They show us how to put our cables around the rails for maximum security and they make sure that the malions (clips or hooks) are closed tight enough so the cables cannot work free. Safety is the prime objective.

While we are waiting, we can see a lot of activity going on all around the set. What really catches us women's attention are some of the workers below. Most don't have shirts on, but there is one that is working in a speedo! We get even, and participate in our own sexual harassment. It was very interesting to say the least. All the women whistling & waving at the speedo man.

Now it is time for us to move. First they take us up to 10° incline and stop so we can get the feel of the set. He asks if anyone feels uncomfortable and those that do not have harnesses are now taken off. Now we go to 25°, we start feeling the pull of gravity and cannot stay on our feet very well. Again we are asked how we are doing. A couple of people want off, so they have to lower the set, unhook them and they get off. Then we begin to go higher. We are laying on the deck now, I have a hold on the rail and my hands are getting sore. We are to look as if we are hanging on to each other, which we really are. Again Simon emphasizes safety and paying attention to "action" and "cut." We are at 43° now, what a rush. I have to let the harness hold my weight because my hands hurt. A stunt man named Chuck is nearby and he keeps an eye on us. CC, Debbie, Robert, Ken, Ralph and I are in a clump at the very top next to the flag pole. I find out that Robert and Ralph go to the same church in Rosarito. We all become one big happy Poop Deck family. Simon tells us to look as if we are struggling for our lives. That is not hard to do given the positions we are in. Simon again wants to know how we are doing and asks for a "thumbs up." No problems, we are having a blast. After practicing the "struggling" a couple more times we come down and head back to wardrobe.

16

We now get dressed for more steerage work in the common room. We are to just wait around again until needed. The second unit is doing this shoot. They are doing a fight scene, where some men get into it and throw each other around into other people, tables and chairs. At one point, they had been working with some of the children and some rats. I heard that the kids were to be playing with them in the corner, but they had to stop because the rat's feet were getting raw on the flooring. It is hot in there again, but this time I have the freedom to stay and watch or go outside. I chose to stay for a while and in between shots I help give water to those that are being used today. I never am used and get wrapped at 7:30 p.m. Debbie Hilton, Anna's mom, follows me to the house and moves in for the next two weeks.

17

October 30, Wednesday

Back to the set at 9:15. We just put our harnesses on and head out to the stern. A storm is moving in from the North. It's cold and windy, a big difference from yesterday. Simon is with us again and the stunt people secure us. We are off to 30º to practice our slip, grab, scream routine. We do "whatever" three times and come down because of the weather.

Back to wardrobe to get another fitting and different shoes. This outfit is a lot nicer and it even smells good. The shoes are sent out to get rubber put on the soles for a better grip on deck. The different outfit is for the harness, in case they need to cut holes in it for the safety cables. My skirt is a light brown print and my blouse is a dark blue. I even get a cape and a scarf that we call a "babushka thingy." We wrap at 2 p.m. and Debbie has to go home, so she takes a list of things we need for the next week. Thermal underwear and thick socks are the most important things that we must have.

Living the Legend: The Journal of a Titanic Background Actress

It's raining now. Hope it clears up before tomorrow because Mr. Cameron wants to start shooting tomorrow night. I can't leave the set yet because I have to call home and nobody is there yet. The rain is coming down hard now, I'm inside the big indoor set. They have begun the flooding shots. I really can't see very much, but I do know that the sitting room has been flooded up to the dining room doors. All that beautiful dining room and sitting room furniture plus the carpet, walls, elevator shafts and Grand Staircase are being ruined. This is ocean water and it is cold, maybe 55°. Everyone has on the thick wetsuits. As they do the shot the whole set moves. Controlled by huge cables that are on each side of the set. The cables suspend the set in the tank and they are attached to the hydraulic motors that lift it up and down and side to side. I am amazed at how fast it can happen. As Cameron yells "action," the man in charge pushes the buttons and brings this massive set to life. It is controlled by a hand held unit that reminds me of the little electric cars that have the wire attached to it. I'm sitting up above the tank, so I can see the operation of the cables as they move. When the filming is going on, everyone must be quiet because the sound carries in the building. When the red lights flash you know to shut-up. If you don't, George (the sound man) will tell you and you don't want George to have to do that….it would be bad.

There is a large wooden walkway that looks like a gang plank that leads down to the top of the set. I can't go down because I am not working. Kate Winslet came through for a moment and said hi and so did Mr. Cameron. He was in his wet suit and got into the jacuzzi to warm up. They are working on the scene where Billy Zane shoots at Leo. They use full load blanks in a 45 caliber hand gun. Even through one deck the sound rings as the gun goes off. They shot this several times and finally break for dinner. I am invited and I am more than glad to raid the crew tent. Really makes me sick to see the great distance between the quality of catering that is there and what we have. I dine on baked sea bass, a variety of salads and desserts. I have an opportunity to visit with the owners of Deluxe Catering and tell them our woes and nightmares with our catering service. He tells me that they originally had the contract for us too, but because of operating regulations in Mexico, they were required to split the contract with the caterers that we had. I asked him to please tell me that they wouldn't have been this bad. He said that the verity would be less, but not the quality. All I could do was moan and smile while thanking him for dinner!

It's still raining as we go back to the set. I meet some new people, Jim Schmidt is one, he works with Mr. Cameron and I have a good time visiting with them all. Simon Crane and Gary sign my book, even Mr. Landau stops and visits for a moment. I say my good nights and head out into the muddy hole that we call a parking lot. It is a horrible mess. They knew that this would happen out here and they could have done something about it, but no, they wait until the problem is worse than ever and we have to deal with it. Almost get stuck, but my trusty truck gets me out. I used to have white tennis shoes, now they are muddy tan. This stuff is like gum, thick, sticky and won't come off until it dries. I have grown two inches in the last 15 minutes. Can't wait to get back to the house, clean up, sit, watch TV and eat the chocolate cake and strawberry cheesecake I took. Yummy! Hanging around has its advantages, off to bed.

18

October 31, Thursday

Back to the set at 10 a.m. It's Halloween, the first time I've been away from home on a holiday. We all are dressed in our street clothes and we have our harnesses on over them. We get up on the stern about 11:30 a.m. The weather is nice again, just a little windy. Jon Landau comes up for a surprise visit, he is dressed as Mr. Potato Head, he is so funny. As he looks around at all of us, he says with surprise, "Where are all your costumes!" We just laugh and point to wardrobe. Oh, how I wish I had my camera to get a shot of him.

We are secured to the rails again, reminded about safety and we are ready to practice our slip, grab, scream routine. We do this three more times and are told that Cameron wants to start shooting Saturday night. We are well prepared for the cold weather with our long underwear.

It's back to wardrobe to finish for the day. Debbie and I are asked to stay and work with a small group for a shooting scene. This is great, we know that the small groups work with Mr. Cameron and actors up close and personal. I jump at the chance. Now we are just sitting around

Living the Legend: The Journal of a Titanic Background Actress

waiting to go in. As we are waiting, Leo comes over and sits near me. He says, "Hello" and I reply the same. He asks how I'm doing tonight and I say fine. As we visit, I can see he doesn't feel well, so my motherly instinct kicks in and I tell him some things that might make him feel better, that my sons, about his age find helpful. He couldn't believe I had boys his age and by then it was time to get busy. It's 9:15 p.m., all we've been able to do is sit near the doorway that opens out to the A Deck Foyer of the Grand Staircase. Here again the detail is exquisite. The staircase is just as the pictures show in the books. The black linoleum patterns that are inlayed in the white are identical. Gold strips of metal that are on the fronts of each stair are real, not just foil or painted on. The engraved woodwork has the same patterns and the color is rich and deep. At the base of each banister, the support rail (newel) posts are adorned with carved wood pineapples. The center hand rail post has a bronze cast lamp, a cherub with wings that is holding over it's head, an upside down, tear drop shaped, white glass globe. The wrought iron railing of the banisters is real metal with what I believe to be gold leafing on the accent pieces. As I stand there waiting and listening I also see the lights on the ceiling. They are exact duplicates to the originals, little crystal beads strung together, larger at the top and taper down as the strands gracefully curve in at the bottom and are attached together with a little gold plated flower. This is the same pattern of the one that was photographed on the wreck that was still hanging from its electric cord, with the feather-like coral growing from it's side. At the top of the staircase is the clock, cherubs on each side, set in an ornately carved frame. The scene is topped off by the beautiful glass dome and it's exquisitely designed wrought iron accents. The light from the roof of the Officer's quarters and the first and second funnels filters down through the opaque panels in the dome. This is a full scale set and you need not try hard to imagine what it was really like as the ship began its plunge of death.

 We are at about a 3-5% forward list. The water is up to the reception room adjoining the dining salon. We are shooting the scene with Billy Zane. Josh greets me and then marries me off to a man named Pete, whose real wife, Nancy, is working in 1st class. His daughter, Shawn and three grandchildren are working on the film, too. Debbie is married off to John-John and given Pete's granddaughter as their own. Cameron is at the top of the stairs. One camera is on a crane looking from above, straight down the side of the staircase, like an overhead shot. Jimmy has the steadycam and precedes Billy down the stairs. Josh places us for the scene. Pete and I are to run across the foyer and then up the stairs, passing the actors in the opposite direction. Debbie and John-John are placed a few steps up from the bottom and run up before us. We were told that there was a gun shot and to act accordingly, but I didn't see who had it. When "action" starts, Kate and Leo start down first. Pete and I run across the foyer and Debbie and John are half way up. Pete and I pass Kate and Leo. On our way up the next flight of stairs, Billy is coming down shouting and when he is a little past us the gun goes off. Cameron had the gun and was leaning over the railing pointing it down the staircase. I was just ahead of Pete, only 5 feet from Cameron as he fired. The sound went through my ear like a knife. I grabbed my ear and leaned against the wall and said quietly, "Oh, thanks for making me go deaf." Mr. Cameron heard me and asked if we had earplugs. We did not and he got very upset that props did not follow his instructions for everyone on set to have them. He knew I was in pain. He said he did not want that kind of thing to happen again to any of us. They got us the plugs and we shot the scene a few more times. The pineapple that adorns the newel post is rigged to explode, so it appears as though it falls victim to one of Billy's bullets. If necessary, props have several ready for reshooting the scene. On one take, Billy is running down the stairs and just as he reaches the bottom trips and twists his ankle. It really hurt and he had to sit a few minutes, before he was able to finish the scene. Pleased with what he films, Mr. Cameron says "Goodnight." We are done at 10 p.m.

19

November 1, Friday

Here I am again at 10:15, out in the north forty mud hole. This is really a stinking mess out here. Some cars can't get through. It's only by shear size and power that I am able to get to the place they want us to park. On my way in I happen to see Zubie. He has been a smiling face to greet us when we get there in the morning and leave at night. He could tell that we are not happy and I am more than glad to tell him the problems out in the parking lot. He said he will speak to transportation later on and see what he could do. I thanked him and told him we would really appreciate any help he could give us.

We are supposed to get our harnesses fitted to our clothing today. So we get dressed just like we are going to for the shoot. We sit around and wait for our turn in the fitting areas. A lot of people have to have holes cut in their costumes so the safety cables can be attached to the harnesses. When it is my turn they discover that I do not require any cutting. So we are done and ready to go by 2 p.m.

Amy, from casting asks if I would be interested in being in the flooded dining room scene. I told her that I would and I thanked her again for thinking of me. My ear is really bothering me and I want the doctor to look at it before I go into the water. I wait around at the top of the indoor set for about 45 minutes. I get to visit with some of the crew and just listen to what is going on inside the dining room. Finally, the doctor can see me, he is really nice and we try to communicate with each other but, he finally has to bring in an interpreter. He looks in my ears and discovers that the one is terribly inflamed, at least it was not burst. He gives me some ear drops and tells me to nurse it as much as possible, keep cotton in it at least a week and use the drops twice a day. After that, I find out that I don't have to stay. So I pack my stuff from the house and head home. Arrive there at 10 p.m.

20

November 3, Sunday

I haven't heard from the studio for 3 days. I start wondering what's happening down there so I call. Good thing I do, because they want us down there tomorrow for a 5 p.m. call. Debbie and I must get packed and coordinate our plans for the morning. We must pack for the week and stop at the Registrar of Voters to get our votes in for election day on the 5th.

It's 1 p.m. and we think we are ready to go. We get about 5 miles down the road and Debbie realizes she has forgotten her cell phone. So, we go back, I can't get upset though, because I had forgotten our cooler of food before I picked her up and had to go back to my place, too. We finally get it together and get to the Clairmont Registrar of Voters at about 2:30. It is packed, we cannot believe how many people are there to make out the absentee ballot. We wait for about half an hour, take care of our civic duty and get to the set by 4:45.

We are to get our Poop Deck clothes on. This is a very interesting process. First, we put on our long underwear. I know what cold night air is like and I have 2 layers. Then the harnesses go on. If I could have filmed this for funniest home videos I would win the $100,000 prize. I didn't have too much trouble, but some of the others were hilarious. Some were putting them on upside down, inside out and backwards. We all finally manage, helping and laughing at each other the whole time. We get up on the deck about 9 p.m. after a long delay for repairs… again. Getting up on the deck is not an easy task either. We must climb a set of stairs that are erected on scaffolding, at least three or four stories up, then once we reach the top, we are helped down about six feet by some of the stunt men and the production assistants. The men have no problem, but, the women have on long skirts, so this boarding process takes a little time. As we get on deck, we see the camera crews setting up for the shot. I start to look around and I hear Josh call me. He is on one side of the deck and I am on the other. He says, "Jude, where are you?" I answer, "Yes, Sir, I'm over here, I'm coming." He can hear me, but doesn't see me because I'm making my way through the crowd. He says "Where?" Rick is near me and points me out to Josh. I emerge from the crowd and Josh says "Good, how you doin, Hon. I want you to stand right here." He puts me up front of a group that is praying with a priest. We have to do a lot of kneeling, so they have to get us knee pads. The scene is intense. The priest is blessing us as we are going down. Jason is next to me. He reaches up to grab the priest's hand and I grab on to Jason's. The priest, played by James Lancaster, is awesome. He is also very funny. As the ship tilts to 15°, people start to slide. We are to look scared and pray out loud, crying and screaming as we go. During the takes, James is intense, he is reciting the "Hail, Mary," as he tries to hold on to us so we don't slip away. After the takes, he lets go of us, and tells us "Get away from me, go to hell, I hope you all die!" He has us in stitches and it certainly breaks the mood of the moment. Especially when he kicks at us for grabbing onto his legs. He is able to rally us back together when the time comes for more. Mr. Cameron is funny, too. He tells us to hold on and not slide until we get to 20°. He thinks we are faking our slide away before that. We tell him that we can't hold on, that we really are sliding away. James tells him that we are pulling his arms off and that he can't hold us that long. So what to do? The prop guys bring in blocks of wood and nail them to the deck so we have a foot hold. Great idea, we are able to deliver exactly what Mr. Cameron wants. Time for a break. Dinner? Don't even ask.

Back on deck. This is our first all nighter and we are all feeling it. Glad I have on plenty of clothes, because it does get cold. Some of my friends learn the hard way and will come better prepared tomorrow night. We start laying around in piles about 3 a.m. We are doing the same thing all night long. The camera angles change, but not what we are doing. Only, now we are praying for the sun to come up! We wrap at 6 a.m. Go home and die.

21

November 5, Tuesday

It's election day. We get to the set at 4 p.m. Debbie is asked to stand in for Linda Kern, one of our Irish actresses. So, she has to go to the set before the rest of us. I don't see her again until dinner. Something has happened to the deck again. They have to hook a big tow truck to the base of the stern to help the hydraulics raise and lower it. Finally, on board about 9:30. We assemble in our prayer group again and do more of what we did last night. Then they decide to make some of us "criers". The make-up folks come on deck and take about six of us to one side. There they paint red make up under our eyes, around our noses and then drop glycerin on our cheeks for tears. It really looks good. People thought we were really crying. Later someone, that didn't know what we had done, asked me if Mr. Cameron had yelled at me and made me cry. I just laughed and said "no way, we have great make-up!" The camera is right behind us. It is on a set of tracks, like a little train. Mr. Cameron tells us to try to stay off of it, because it won't let the camera move properly. As we finally do get to 20° we have nothing to hold onto except the priest again. When we were at 15° it was hard, but it is really bad now. Props has to give us back our wooden blocks, because we can't stay off the tracks. As the scene begins, James, the priest, begins his lines. The camera moves back and forth in order to capture the fear in his face. We are praying and sobbing, following his lead. The next scene the camera is facing us. Cameron has his hand held camera for these scenes. We do the same thing for him. He wants to capture our fear now.

Later, he focuses his attention on the prayer group again. They have removed the tracks and that's when the fun really begins. We try, once again, to hold on as long as possible. Lucy is behind me. She has a hold of my cape. As we begin to slide, she starts to choke me. All of this happens really fast. She keeps her grip until the group piles up at the end of the deck. As I tell her what she is doing to me, I realize that the heel of my shoe has come off and that four sharp nails are exposed and I stick myself with them. I tell everyone to be careful, we can't move until they lower the deck. I tell someone that I can't move or I'll hurt someone. A couple of the crew help me up and the prop guys get some good old electrical tape and get me back in action. We set again and I tell Lucy where to grab me so she doesn't hurt me again. I guess she didn't understand and she does the same thing, three more times! The last shot I got a little upset and this time it sinks in and it works fine. The priest is holding on, Jason grabs him, I grab Jason, and everyone else grabs us. As "Forgive all their trespasses" is said we reach 20°, and not being able to hold on any longer we slide to our demise. Now Mr. Cameron wants something different. When we reach the bottom, we are screaming, we are to pause. The upward tilt has stopped. The stern has broken free from the rest of the ship and has fallen back down to be level once again. As we think we will be safe now, we react with great excitement and grab hold of each other and proclaim, "We are saved!" Then it all starts again as quickly as it ends and we all realize that we are sinking faster then ever as we reach 90° and plunge beneath the sea. After we perform our part, the prayer group wraps at 4:30 a.m. but, do I get to go home and sleep? No, I get to drive Debbie back to the border so she can get a ride back home. It is an hour and a half round trip to the border and back to the house. I crawl into bed about 6:30 a.m.

22

November 6, Wednesday

~~~~~~~~~~~~~

As I try to sleep, the world around me is stirring. I keep getting woke up. The caretaker of the property keeps pounding on something. As can be imagined, I am not a happy camper and want to go pound on him. I resort to my earplugs instead.

To the set at 4 p.m. It's pretty windy. The other nights we have been out here, these helium filled balloon lights, that we call the sun and moon, have been up. So have these huge 75 x 150 feet black backdrop screens that are held up by huge cranes (which I hate). The cranes make me very uncomfortable. Well, the lights and the screens are down. After a little waiting around, we get up on deck and assemble along the rails. It's about 7 p.m. and it's still windy. On the top of one of the taller cranes is a flag. We can see how windy it is. One of the men in our group owns a boat and estimates it to be between 15 and 20 mph. They go ahead and put the lights back up. There are three of them, two on the docking bridge and one on a lift basket (cherry picker) next to the set. The one up on the cherry picker is very entertaining as the wind proceeds to move that one the most. There is a very brave man in that basket and we watch the balloon beat him up. He literally is laying down at times to avoid the movement of this thing that is at least 6 feet in diameter. The basket itself is being bounced around like a bucking horse. The wind must be stronger now because these things are really wiping around. All of a sudden, the light that is closest to us starts to break loose. We hear the popping of the cables and turn just in time to see it being taken instantly into the sky. The only thing that keeps this $15,000 light from becoming the "Titanic Satellite" is its power line. It goes up and out about 250 feet and it takes five men to pull it back down. After that, the real fun begins. We reassemble our prayer group. Mr. Cameron wants to get a couple more shots like the night before. After that we get moved over to the left hand side of the stern. We call this area the dummy corner, because we aren't supposed to be seen anymore. They have put the big screens back up, because the winds have seemingly calmed down. As we are standing at the rails, waiting for another take, the wind kicks up again. There is a black skirt that has been attached to the bottom of the big screen and is just hanging there loosely and is about six feet tall. It runs the length of the screen and it's purpose is to cover the lights and equipment that are in that area behind it. Well, it tears right off and the guys come over and start replacing it. It is really quiet and eerie, then all of a sudden, you could hear the wind coming, like a freight train, from the northeast, through the big set buildings and the construction site, straight at us. The wind catches the screen like a big sail, the crane starts to creak and moan. You could hear the metal frame of the screen grinding and we could see it start to buckle. The men below start hollering up "get those people out of there!" Now, you must realize that we have been tied to the rails with our safety lines, so we can't move. The screen starts to swing towards the ship and only stops when the bottom of it hits a dirt burm and some background lighting. When it hit the lights, it started a little fire, but fortunately extinguished itself, quickly. By that time we have gotten ourselves loose and away from that side of the stern. Our big fear is not that screen, it is the crane that is holding it. We can see it moving around, straining and can hear it creaking, the support cables were making noise but, didn't snap. All of the black material that is attached to the frame rips and shreds to pieces. Cameron orders everyone abandon ship. Despite what was happening we did not panic and got off in a very orderly manner. They finally get the screen under control and lay it on the ground. We are able to see the damage that is done to the frame, all twisted and bent. We wonder if it can be fixed. During this time the special effects green screen survives the wind attack. It is the same size as the others, but it is sitting about 30 feet down in the empty water tank directly in front of the stern set. We go back up and do a few more takes and wrap at 5:30 a.m. Boy, are we glad that is over.

23

November 7, Thursday

It's still windy as I arrive at the set at 4:15 p.m. Not only is it causing problems down here, I call home and find out my horse has gotten out. Thank God, our neighbor came over and helped my husband catch him.

Up to the deck for another wild night. As I was getting ready, I notice that Barbara, one of our older ladies, is not here. I later find out that she fell last night on the stairs and broke her finger. They wouldn't let her back on set with the injury. I sure do miss her, I know how much she wants to be here.

They have both screens up again. They were able to repair the frame and hang new material. Now they have a smaller screen hung between the larger ones and secured to the ground with rebar stakes. They all form an "L" shape around the set area. We are still in the dummy corner. We are at a 25° tilt. This has been the usual filming angle for awhile and that is why we must use our safety lines. Although the stunt people have secured us again, those of us in the dummy corner make sure that we can easily get free if something happens tonight. Last night the ends of my line were screwed so tight that I couldn't get loose and when the trouble started and the men said to get out of there. I hollered, "We can't get out of here, we're tied to the stinking rail!!" It's windy and a little cold. We joke with each other and wonder how long the screens will last. It doesn't take long for that question to be answered. Here comes the wind, almost like last night. A dead calm around the set, in the distance, the sound of a freight train approaching. We stop and watch, fingers ready to loosen the malions. It hits the big screen first and moves it around, then the little screen is torn loose from the stakes in the ground. It whips up towards us and with it comes dirt and little pieces of gravel. Some of us drop to our knees and I can feel the dirt hit my face as I close my eyes. I holler "Duck!!" and undo myself. The canvas is snapping about three to four feet away from our faces. As we begin to stand up, the top corner of the black screen tears downward and then the rest of it follows, like peeling a banana. They had made it a tear away so the frame wouldn't bend again. Off the ship we go and it is a little worse than last night. They lay the other screens down when there is another lull. For some reason, I guess because they thought it was safe last night, they leave the green screen up. Ten minutes later, it starts to shred and it goes down. I sure would hate to be the one that made that decision. We heard it cost $50,000.00.

After awhile, we do go back up and shoot different angles. Scenes mostly of Kate and Leo at the very end of the stern. We can't see a lot, but we do entertain each other. Ellen still has her ugly baby. A couple of the men ask to see it. As she hands it to them, they look it over and do the usual abuse that it has suffered many times. Such as getting its face mashed in and pinching its cheeks together. Then they decide to try something new. One of guys takes his belt and wraps it around its neck. Then he proceeds to dangle it over the side of the deck. Provoking an unruly response of cheers from our deviant group and much laughter from the crew below us on the ground.

The stunt crew does some of their work tonight also, rolling down the deck and into various objects that have been prepared for their impact. We call it the "Nurf" set, but even with the padding and rehearsal of their falls, three stunt people get hurt. A broken ankle, a couple bruised

23

ribs, and a gashed eye. These people are incredible and it is awesome to be able to watch them. We feel really bad when one gets hurt, but they all take it in stride. I'm also getting to know a few of them by name and they are getting used to working around us because we have to stay in our spots as they work. We are not allowed to participate in the stunts, but we are to look like we are part of it. It's hard to describe and we are told it looks great. We shoot right to sun-up.

24

November 8, Friday

I got four hours of sleep and headed home to pick up Jeff. They called and told him he might work tonight. We get to the set at 4:15 p.m. It is not as windy and it sure is warm. I don't have to put all my layers of clothes on. We are experiencing a good Santa Ana condition. This lets us shoot without the possibility of fog all night long.

We thought they wouldn't try to put up any of the screens. But no, they try to raise another green screen. I guess the shooting schedule calls for it. We watch and wonder as they begin to raise it up with one of the cranes. Here it comes again, the wind. They are caught off guard and the wind catches it like a big sail and shoves it into a generator box along with some men on the ground. Fortunately, no one is hurt. We exit the ship again. As we walk by the screen we can see about an 8 x 8 foot section torn from hitting the generator box. As we are waiting around they do more stunt work and only one stunt man gets hurt tonight. I start to visit with a man that is in charge of the generators and lighting. We go and have dinner with him and have a good time talking about all that is going on around the set. He tells of some of the films he has worked on before, like "Alligator".

We go back up on deck and try to act as if we are fighting our way to the top of the stern. I have to remove my cape and scarf so I will look different. We shoot to dawn again and go the Don Luis Hotel.

25

November 9, Saturday

Up at 4 p.m. to the studio at 5:15. Jeff is on stand-by so he gets paid. The deck is set up for the stunt people so they can do the 90° stuff, like falling. They have a new plan for the screens. They set them up back to back like a big "A" frame. Great idea but, there is no wind tonight. It is warm again and we are able to watch some of the excitement. The stunt people are on cables, trying to simulate falling. As time goes by, we break for lunch and they can't lower the deck. It's stuck again, but, this time with about 100 stunt people, along with Jon Landau's wife and son. They were in no danger, plus everyone had harness on. They just had to hang around for about an hour as they fixed the mechanism again. Finally, they are all down. Don't know what is going on, but all we do for the rest of the night is sit around and tell jokes. We really have a great time. We wrap at 2:30 a.m. and head for home. We arrive there at about 4:30, sleep until 11 or so and just relax. I get a call telling me to be back to the set again on Monday the 11th, at 4 p.m. I also get a phone call from one of the lighting guys. He lives in Phoenix,

Arizona and had flown home for the weekend. He wanted to know if I could pick him up at the San Diego Airport. No problem, I just stopped on my way down to the set and we arrive at the studio at 3:30 p.m. I grabbed some goodies at the crew tent and checked in at 4.

Now here we are again, just sitting around watching the stunt people do their thing. They have been doing the jumps from the side of the Poop Deck. When they jump, they fall into stacks of empty cardboard boxes that have a layer of padding on top. I had always thought they used big thick foam pads for that type of fall. They used the airbag type when the falls were higher up. It is 9:45 and still not doing anything. What a drag. We wrap at 3 a.m. I take Sandy & Chris to the Don Luis. No one is tired so some others get together and we all go to this little bar. We sit and talk, watch some guys play pool and head back to the hotel at 5:15.

26

November 12, Tuesday

Back to the set at 4 p.m. The fog rolls in early and it is thick. The man that runs the big lighting truck, informs us that the lights on his truck are useless at the distance he has them set (approx. 300 yards) These lights are on a huge rack, which extends to different heights up to 150 feet, there are 15 of them and they are like the lights at a football stadium. Extremely powerful, and they are useless! That gives you the idea of how thick the fog was. It's cold, that wet, piercing cold. We have nothing to do but wait.

As the night progresses…we don't. Bo comes in the tent and asks us who got 10's on their tests in T.J. These are the tests we took while Simon Crane observed us. The screaming, tumbling, and swimming was about to get rewarded. She asks us to get together with her inside the ladies dressing area for a meeting. She wants to know if we want to go up on deck and turn to 90°, because they need more people up there to thicken the crowd. We all want to go! This is about 3 a.m. and they let everyone else go home. We have to stay, hoping they will call us up on deck. We end up doing nothing and getting wrapped at 4:30. It is hard and slow driving those 5 miles back to the house. The fog is so thick I can only drive about 10 mph. On my way I see lights on the side of the road. It is one of our buses. It apparently has had an accident with a car. I go by and there was no one except the driver on board. Thank God there is no traffic at this hour.

27

November 13, Wednesday

We get to the set again at 4 p.m. After doing nothing for three nights & watching numerous times of the deck getting stuck, we are finally summoned. I'm greeted by Mr. Cameron, Sebastian and Josh again. It was good to be able to do something, and to be told you were missed. I told them I missed them too, and that I was glad to be back on deck. We thought the fog might roll in again, but it stayed clear.

We are lined up along the bottom rail. Chris, Lance and I are close together. They assemble a ramp next to me that is covered with dummies. They place Leo's double, Joey, on top. They start to turn the deck, it doesn't go too fast. You can hear everything creaking, but it is smooth. We reach 45°, 55°, 75°, the whole time feeling different sensations of gravity as we go. We are actually laying on our backs and sides on the railing. Now we are at 90°, completely straight up and down, two feet above the green screen that is under us. All the stunt people are dangling in various places over us, some as high as 150 feet. We are to look as if we are falling, waving our arms and legs. Oh yeah, don't forget the screaming. The ramp I'm next to is to look like a pile of people, crammed together as the ship sinks. It is also a launching pad for the stunt people to bounce off of. In between takes, one of the stuntmen takes our picture as we pose in our screaming, grabbing & crying routine. It does start to get cold, but I'm ready for it tonight. After a while we turn back down again and they rearrange us along the side railings. I get stuck between two of our bigger guys and several other people. It is very tight. They turn us up to 60° and I discover that I'm getting crushed, they have to go back down to reposition us. Chuck (a stuntman) makes fun of me, because he has to help me out of where I'm at and hook me up again. He says "I should have known it was you causing trouble over here." We laugh as we find a better place. A few more takes at this position, then we go back to where we were before and more 90° shots. As we are waiting for another take, we notice Linda Hamilton watching us up on the edge of the pit we are in. She had brought their (her & Mr. Cameron's) little girl. He was up in his basket, filming the top of the Poop Deck. They had moved over by the video monitors, and someone gave her a microphone and over the load speakers, she says "Hi, Daddy, I love you." He replied, "I love you too, Honey." She was so cute. We do a couple more shots and we are asked to get off.

As we are waiting around, I briefly meet and talk to Linda Hamilton. She was very nice and said that she just wanted to come and watch the action. She wanted to know how we were holding up. Then she had to go. I went into the crew tent again and got some water, which I thought we could do, but no. I get in trouble for that. I just don't get the separation of tents, especially when ours is filled with crap. Well, I'll never do that again, don't need anyone mad at me or need to get anyone in trouble. So, I'll do my part to keep the peace. We go back up for one more turn to 90° and then wrap at 6 a.m. I go home and get five days to recoup. We start Southampton on Monday.

28

November 18, Monday

This is going to be the most difficult part of the shoot so far. I would rather be back in the tank again than do what I have to do to get to the set. Even though I am staying five miles away from the set, casting wants me to drive to T.J. 40 minutes north to catch a stupid bus and then ride back to the set another hour or better. They go through a maze of back streets to get down to the set so they don't have to pay the toll on the good highway. I leave my house at 1:15 a.m. so I can be at Senior Taco's at 2:30. I check in on my bus, and we leave a little after 3. The bus is cold, no heat, and the road? God only knows. It's dark, I figure if we crash I don't want to see what we're hitting anyway. Get to the set at about 4:30. Once the sun comes up, we see that the Poop Deck is gone. To our amazement we see that it has been put up on scaffolding and reattached to the ship. I would have liked to have seen that job done. It was moved in one piece. I see Bo in the middle isle of wardrobe. As we start to talk, we hear this horrendous crash from outside. We look at each other in horror, thinking the same thing…that the Poop Deck had just collapsed. We and some others run to the door that leads out to the set lot. As we throw open the double doors, expecting to see the worst, we are relieved to see that it is just a trash truck that is dropping off some 20 foot dumpsters.

They are expecting 1500 people on the set today. Everything for signing in is different. Things seem to be going smoothly. They have several tents set up for us to have our meals in. Those of us that know the routine, help those that are new. We do our best to help out. We get out to the set at 8 a.m. We watch Mr. Cameron set up for the shots he wants. Everyone is hurrying around because of the light situation. He wants to take advantage of the sun. We finally start about 10:30 and do a lot by our 12:30 break. We are moving around on the dock, acting like we don't know what to do to get on board. They have horses and buggies, cars and dock workers trying to get through the crowds to their destinations. Ellen gets to ride in one of the old cars, she is photo double for Frances Fisher, so we don't see each other very much. Barbara and I have sort of teamed up. We do a good "wandering around" routine. After break, we do a lot of waiting around. I get to sleep for about 10 minutes and then back out on the dock for more scenes. With all the moving around I observe many details that I doubt will ever be seen on film. All the print on everything is backwards, even the labels on the luggage and the plates on the ground near the bollards on the dock.

We get to wrap at 5 p.m. It takes over an hour to get back to T.J. Sandy decides to stay with me, and we get lost trying to get back out of T.J. to the road to Rosarito. Finally get to bed by 9 p.m.

29

November 19, Tuesday

We get up at 1:30 a.m., miss the T.J. bus and have to go to Rosarito to take that one. At least it was easier on us. We check in with our bus captains and no one cares. It's windy and cold today. We arrive on set at 4:15 a.m.

Scott and Ethen are back helping in casting again. They have been gone and it is nice to have them back. New people have dubbed the film "Satanic", figures the problem makers would say that. Sure wish someone would get upset over our eating situation. Haven't had anything for two days, glad I brought some yogurt. Oh well, I need to lose weight, this is good therapy.

Back to the set, to find a big hoop-la. Several people got upset and took their meal up to the crew tent and showed Josh what we were getting. Our wish has come true, Mr. Cameron and Josh are livid. They can not believe what they are seeing and hearing, they didn't know how bad it was. They say things will change. After that everyone settles down and back we go to do a little more crowd scenes and then wrap at 5 p.m.

I have the pleasure of being on a bus that has a toilet in it. I don't have to tell you what that smelled like. I don't care if I do get in trouble, I won't do that again. I'm driving in. This bus system wasn't set up for those of us that have been here all along. It was set up for crowd management just for the Southampton shoot. After I get back to the house, I watch some of the TV Titanic. It is really lame compared to ours. It's funny how many people back home thought this is what we have been down here doing. To bed by 8:45 and I wonder what tomorrow will bring.

30

November 20, Wednesday

―――※―――

Miss all the buses, drive to the set and get in with no problems. The guys at the gate know me by now and just wave. A lot of people have quit, and there are not enough to fill the demand. I have heard they are sending busses into town to recruit people off the street so we have enough for the scenes.

Back out on the set and get into our positions. Barb and I are up on the gangway together. A friend takes a couple of good pictures. It is a fake ramp that looks like it is going into the side of the ship. We actually walk across it then go down a couple of steps and move out of camera range, we never actually go into the ship from here. I see Jim Schmidt again, he is in costume. He is dressed like one of the inspectors that are checking people for lice before they can get on board. He looks great, I love a man in uniform. I have also discovered that he is more then just a consultant to Mr. Cameron, he said he is actually Mr. C's bodyguard. In light of the resent kidnapping of the Sony officials, they feel this is necessary. They don't want to take any chances. Can't say that I blame them. We see guards posted around the set with rifles, too. We have our own little fort on the beach.

We get to go up on the deck today. They show us how and where to go for the next series of scenes. Do a quick exploring walk, but will take more time later. It really is amazing. Everything that I have seen in pictures and drawings has come to life right before my eyes. It is beautiful, the decks, lifeboats, wheel house, the small details of the signs and lighting, from what I know, it is all here.

We have our break and things have not improved. A lot are upset and go on another visit to the crew tent, raw chicken in hand. We have another conference and our raffle today. Lance won $100, some guy that was only there his 1st day won the $500, we don't even know who he was. I wasn't here the last time they had the raffle, Ken won the $500 that time. It is good that they have come up with a special event now and then to encourage us. They have given away T-shirts, and other movie goodies along with the money rewards. I would like to collect on Mr. Cameron's promise, that if we had another bad meal he would take us to lunch at Carl's Jr.

Now it is back to shooting. Sebastian picks a few of us to go inside the ship. There is a little room set up to appear as the entrance to the 3rd Class areas located near the stern of the ship. We are to stand in or near the gang way door and wave good-bye to those on the dock. We are setting the scene for Leo and Danny to run on board just before the gang way is removed. There are about 10 of us, but with the camera and lighting crews we are really crammed in there. In between shots I visit a little with Shelley, she keeps the notes for the script. It looks tedious, but she enjoys it. It is starting to get dark and we wrap at 5:30. I go home and watch the rest of the other "Titanic".

31

November 21, Thursday

On set at 4 a.m. and it is cold. We are trying to recreate the scene from the first day when Kate and Billy arrive on the dock. Only this time on the opposite end of the set. All the time we have been doing this we have been around horses and moving objects. It amazes me of the stupidity of some of these people. They act like they have no clue on how to move out of the way of something that is obviously larger and stronger then they are. If you don't pay attention to your surroundings how can someone else do it for you? I guess after being raised on a ranch I'm a bit unforgiving when it comes to safety around horses. People were cautioned everyday about this. The buggies move rapidly and sometimes in a confined area. Horses tend to get a little apprehensive, no matter how well they are trained, when surrounded by crowds for long periods of time they can get claustrophobic so to speak. Anyway, people would get too close and touch where they shouldn't touch and end up getting stepped on or their toes run over.

Dario is my "husband" today. We stand off to one side for a shot or two. Then Josh calls Dario and Linda. I turned to see Linda and she wasn't there. I was by myself. Realizing that Josh really wanted me, I have to run to catch up. I kind of laugh to some of our friends as I pass. As I finally catch up, Josh sees me laughing. I guess he thinks I am laughing at his instructions and does not like that one bit. He looks at me and is very angry. As he looks down at me, he shouts "Do you think this is funny?!" I am a little afraid, and respond, "No Josh, but I'm not Linda, I'm Jude, remember?" He just stops for a moment and holds my arm, he replies, much calmer "I'm sorry. Just stand here for awhile." All day things have not gone right. Earlier, I had heard Josh speaking to Jon Landau and he did not sound happy about something. Now we are to walk down the side of one of the old cars, a 1912 Rambler. Dario guides me through the crowd as we look at the luggage in the car. There are other cars on the dock, too. A blue Rolls Royce that was said to have belonged to the Czar of Russia, and valued at 1 million dollars. Another car, that you will see being loaded on to the ship. The owner of that one said it was the most expensive whorehouse ever made. We asked what he meant and he said it was valued at $350,000 and modified so one side comes off for filming the love scene. We do the "walk by the car" scene a few times. After that we form a line that supposedly goes into the ship. We do that a lot, then break for lunch. Bo and I visit with each other and I let her know that lunch isn't half bad today. She thanked me for telling her that and says, "I'll talk to you later, Linda." I laugh and tell her what had happened earlier with Josh, that he called me Linda too. Weird. Things were a bit "tiffy" on the set earlier, I guess it messed everybody up.

It starts drizzling about 2:30 p.m. Thought we would wrap because all the costumes are getting wet and wardrobe is not happy about that. But Mr. Cameron wants to get more shots of what we did the night before. I find a semi-dry area to wait in, I get a little cold. This goes on until 6:00. Because it is raining, we have been told to stay in the tents, especially those that are wearing 1st Class outfits. We have also been told not to walk back to the wardrobe building, we were to stay in the tents until buses came for us. Yvette is trying to keep everyone inside and this process takes a long time. So the people that have only been there for this shoot start getting impatient and don't want to do what they are told. They keep crowding out the entrance of the tent. They remind me of turkeys that want to look up at the rain and then end up drowning themselves. I guess they think that it will make the buses get there faster. Yvette keeps telling them to get back. Now she can't talk as loud as I can, so I begin to help her and tell everyone to please cooperate and get out of the rain because it is ruining certain outfits. We start moving them back in and I hear someone say "Stop treating us like cattle." With that I say "Stop acting stupid like cattle and do what you've have been asked!" Yvette thanked me. As we finally get on the bus, this one lady starts complaining that I don't understand how uncomfortable she is in her semi damp outfit. I said "You won't get any sympathy from me. I've been here from the beginning and have been in more water than you'll ever see." Her whole attitude changed and she says "Oh, I guess you would know then." I told her that not cooperating with the production crew only makes it harder for us. Back at wardrobe, get changed and head out. I hear it's supposed to rain all night. I get to bed by 8.

32

November 22, Friday

It does rain all night. Up at 4 a.m. and I look outside to see it is still coming down hard. I go back to bed until 6. It seems to have stopped. Get to the set at 7:30. The parking lot is really a mess. Some people get stuck trying to park, which creates a whole new problem for many people.

We are still shooting the dock scenes. We are very deep background, just moving bodies for the effect. We have been doing a lot of waiting because they are shooting Kate, Billy and all the other primary people getting on the ship. I go up to one of the buggies that's stuck in the rear with us and meet the driver. He lets me get up on it with him. No sooner do I get comfortable, they decide to get us moving again. So it's back to background again. The sun comes out off and on and dries things out a bit. We are now supposed get up on the rear Well Deck, just in front of the Poop Deck. This is a job in itself, just getting up there. Things are still being constructed and we have to be very careful. The rain has warped some of the decking, so we must watch where we walk so we don't trip. On top of that, they have just painted a lot of the railings with oil paint instead of water based paint. It is not drying and people are getting this orange brown paint all over there costumes as we try to do what we are told. We are on the rail waving good-bye. We don't do much else, but walk back and forth. It is really cool to see everyone down below us moving around on the dock. We can see everything, even the path all the buggies and cars take when they move around the set for another take. We can see how big our "ocean" will be. All the dock and building facades will be removed and this entire six acres will be filled with water. There is a moat around the ship that is deeper, that has been filled already to appear as if the ship were at dock. It runs the length of the ship. From the stern it is about 20 feet deep and as it gets to the forward Well Deck drops to about 45 + feet to accommodated the sinking effects that are still to come. It's really amazing the planning that has gone into this set. We wrap at 5:30 p.m. go get dressed and go out to a birthday party for one of the office girls, have a great time dancing ourselves to death and to bed by 10:30 p.m.

33

November 23, Saturday

To the set and up on the bow by 8 a.m. Again we have to contend with painted surfaces. I don't know why they didn't use water based paint. It would have saved a lot of grief. We are to wave good-bye again. There is a big platform with a forklift at one end down on the dock. It looks to be about 25 x 25 feet. Behind it is a long track for the camera to be pushed on. As action begins and we are waving, they actually push the platform with the people and a car along the side of the ship to give the feeling the ship is moving away from the dock. We do that a few times and then go back down on the dock, where we are once again exiled to deep background by the stern.

After break, we go to the Well Deck to shoot the seen where Kate and Leo first make eye contact. Now we start having fun, or should I say, we go insane. We watch the camera crews set up on the Poop Deck, the lighting and all that is on the Promenade Deck, both of which are higher then the Well Deck. so we are looking up at all of this activity. Leo and Danny are seated at the railing on the Poop Deck. They are discussing Leo's art work. Kate, caddie corner from them, walks out on the back of the Promenade to watch the sunset. As she makes her first appearance, she has this big flat-rimmed sun hat on. The crown is squared and covered with what looks like orange flowers and some sheer fabric over those. It looks like a big salad on a pizza. We all laugh among ourselves as we see this coming. Mr. Cameron has the same reaction over the PA system. "Kate, what the hell is that on your head?" she replies "I don't know, but I feel like an eff-ing pizzeria. It's dammed ugly isn't it?" We all laugh at that one. They try to correct it, but to no avail. The hat is axed, never to be seen again. Our part in this is simple, we are to move into groups, watch children play, or just walk over to the rails to watch the sunset. Sandy, Chris and I have our own entertainment going in our group. We are standing under one of the deck cranes. I am able to examine this piece of equipment more closely and discover that everything that should be metal is actually wood. During this inspection, the part that looks like a pulley comes apart and swings down like a big pendulum. It's heavy so it swings quickly. I jump back with a gasp, others turn in time to avoid getting conked. We stick the piece back together and tell props. I think they fixed it with wood glue. We are acting like we are having a light hearted conversation. Smiling and nodding at each other, we are discussing where we have all come from. I say, I am from Mongolia, I found my husband cheating and killed him. I stole his family fortune. I am traveling 3rd Class so I will not be discovered. I am going to America to start a new business. I will sell, Bat Bait Bagels with bacon, butter and beans, by the bag or by the box in Boston. It is not hard for us to appear that we are happy and having a good time. We have this conversation a few times and then wrap at 6:30. I head for home and arrive at 9:30 p.m. Because of an early call on Monday, I leave Sunday evening and get back to Rosarito by 9:30 p.m.

34

November 25, Monday

We are up on the Well Deck by 7:30 a.m. It has been sunny out and we are to wear sun screen all the time. We can't get sun burned or we will be to dark for the other shots to come. They want us really white I guess. We sit and watch anything and everything. Lunch at 3:30 and it wasn't half bad. In fact it's been pretty good for three days now. We sit around some more and after a very boring day, wrap at 5:30 p.m. I go have dinner with Ellen, Chris and Sandy at El Patio. Off to bed by 9:30.

November 26, Tuesday. To the set at 5:30 a.m. again. The crew is up on the Well Deck again. We really don't do a whole lot, we don't even get up on the ship. It's really hard when we don't get to do anything. We entertain ourselves by walking around and seeing what changes have been made on all the sets for the up coming scenes. I like to talk to new people and see what they are doing for the film. The crew has been really fun to get to know.

Living the Legend: The Journal of a Titanic Background Actress

What a day. Because of the lack of people, the buses are sent into town to pick up people wanting to work. Unfortunately, they can't screen them and they don't know what they may be getting or bringing back for us to deal with. As we were having lunch, one of our regulars over hears a young guy soliciting one of our seven year old boys. Telling him how to make money with naked pictures and asking if he wants to see the showers in the men's room. This guy is immediately stopped from talking to the child and the little boy's mother is alerted to what is happening. Some of the men stop the guy from leaving and security is alerted. He is very lucky to have gotten out of our tent in one piece. He was taken away, never to return. It must be weirdo day, because it doesn't end there. About an hour after that incident, there is some strange guy over making lude gestures and comments to the make-up girls. This time security and the police are called. This guy is big and they don't want to provoke him. He has been around all day and was asked several times by the head of the make-up department to leave. He is now seeing butterflies and talking to himself. They finally get him outside of the building and take him away. We never discover what happened to either of these people after they left our area. We wrap around 6 p.m. and go to dinner again. Then to bed at 10:30.

November 27, Wednesday. Get to the set at 7:30 a.m. Find out that I am not needed to work today. So I go back to the house, clean up and get back to San Marcos around 1 p.m. Tomorrow is Thanksgiving, glad to be home.

Spend Thanksgiving with family and go down to the set the day after with my sons and husband. We get a special tour of the set with Zubie, get to go up on the ship and show them all the things that we have worked on already. As we are walking around the Boat Deck, we stop and look at the lifeboat davits. All the ones on the right side of the ship are real. Only the first four on the other side are. The rest are made of wood and plastic. They were made by the same company that made them for the real "Titanic" back in 1912. If I remember correctly, these are valued at $40,000 a pair. I'm sure the originals were just a fraction of that cost. We are able to wander around and look just about everywhere. Further inspection of the machinery on the deck reveal that they are made of plastic, wood and fiberglass. Exceptional detail makes it hard to tell unless you touch or look very close at things. I'm so grateful that we are able to experience this together. It gives them all a deep appreciation for what is happening here. Later, I introduce them to some of our friends and finish the day with dinner at El Patio. They loved it.

35

December 2, Tuesday

It's been 5 days and it seems like a month. Finally got a call to be in today at 6 a.m. They want Jeff to work, too. This will be fun to have my son with me. We get up at 4:00 a.m. and arrive on time. Up to the set by 7:30. We will be working with the second unit, special effects team. We go up on the forward Well Deck, between the bow and the bridge. They place us on the rail. The camera is on a long track a little behind the large group of people watching the ship leave dock. We are to be waving at the crowd and I guess to give a different sense of movement, they push the camera along the track. As we wave we are to pick someone out on the dock below and wave directly at them. We are yelling good-bye, we'll miss you, things like that. Well, no one can really hear us, so we decide to say our own things. I choose to say, "Good-bye, I hate your guts, I took all your money and I hope you all die!" Others choose to be a bit more vulgar. We do this about six times. After that, they put us on the dock and do some more waving. It is our responsibility to remember where we might possibly be seen and not get into shots that would be out of sync with what has already been done. I have been seen on the ship already, so I can't be in with the close up shot on the crowd that is watching the ship leave. So we just sit off to the side and try to stay warm. Even though the sun is out, it's freezing in the shade. We just watch a group stand in front of a large green screen and wave at it. We wrap at around 4 p.m. and then go to dinner at El Patio with Ellen. After dinner we stop back at the set and watch some of the set up of lights and equipment around the ship. It is very interesting to see the behind the scenes prep. I never knew what was involved before and this makes me appreciate what we are doing a lot more. We don't work tomorrow, so we will go home in the morning.

36

December 10, Tuesday

Haven't been needed at the set for seven days. They have been doing 1st Class stuff again. I finally get a call this morning at 9 a.m. to be on the set at 2:15 p.m. this afternoon. I could have used one more day to decorate the house, but I got a lot done this last week so I'm not worried. I hurry and get on the road by noon, go to the house, unpack and arrive on the set right on time. Boy, what a surprise I get. The Southampton dock and all the buildings are gone! All the stuff that was in the tank area is gone. The only thing in there now is the tower crane and sea water. What an awesome effect "Titanic" is at sea! There is a soft breeze from the north, cold, but not too uncomfortable. As the sun sets, all the lights are a blaze and she has come to life. Magnificent is the only description of what I see.

I greet everyone and catch up on what's been going on. I can't believe all that has changed in just a week. I get my hair and make-up done, but never get dressed. There are a lot of people on the set for the first time tonight, mostly 1st Class. There are groups of people that need to go to the set and there are not enough assistants to escort them. I have been asking if I could help with anything and tonight they take me up on my offer. I take at least four groups of people to the holding area on the ship. There is an elevator located in the center of the ship, between the second and third funnels. I estimate it to be about nine stories up. There are sets of stairs that go up also. I have used them a couple of times when I haven't been in a hurry.

I don't dress for filming all night. I wander around and watch some of the lighting guys work on a rack of lights that is supposed to be up on the tower crane. I guess they were working before, so they had sent the original technician that set them up back to the States. After watching them fuss and fume over the problem for a while, I return to our lair. We are all sitting around inside the wardrobe building, it's to cold in the tent. They can't seem to keep propane on hand for the heaters. Julian brought in some weird puzzle that we must have worked on for a couple of hours and just as we finish, they wrap us at 1 a.m. Get to sleep a little more tonight.

December 11, Wednesday. To the set at 2:30 p.m. We get up on the stern about 4:00. We do background for Kate and Leo as they are talking to each other and are spitting off of A Deck. We move back and forth, stop at the rail and look at the sunset. We actually see real dolphins out in the ocean. There are four of them side by side in a wave and it looks like they are body surfing. We are only up there for about an hour and then we lose the sunset. On my way down they tell me to go get refitted for 1st Class. I couldn't believe it. I didn't think I would ever get to change. I'm so excited and everyone could hardly wait to see what I look like. The outfit is maroon, it has long sleeves, with black velvet cuffs. It is three pieces, skirt, jacket and a black velvet dickey under that, that has a high collar of lace. It is not fancy 1st Class, we call it casual 1st Class. I go to make up and get "nice" this time. Now I go to hair and they put it up, kind of rolled up on each side. Not exactly what I had hoped, but it will do for tonight. I'm told to hurry up to the ship. Everyone is already there. We are assembled out on the Boat Deck, just moving around near the 1st Class gym entrance. I go out on the deck to present myself to all those that have seen me trashy for 2½ months. No one can believe it. Dario is the funniest, he turned and looked at me

36

in amazement, he said, "Judy, you are beautiful." Sebastian asked me why I left my poor cousin in 3rd Class. Everyone is impressed. It is cold and wet out, a fine drizzle settles on all of us, glad I brought my long underwear again. Now we just walk around in deep background until 6:30 a.m.

37

December 12, Thursday

We don't have to be to the set until 5:30 p.m. I am told to dress 1st Class again. They take a little more time with my hair and it looks more like what I had envisioned, like Barbara Streisand in "Hello Dolly". We are to start shooting inside, near the Grand Staircase. Josh sees me and smiles, saying "They finally moved you to 1st Class, hey Jude?" He was in a really good mood. I just said "Yeah, finally." Mr. Cameron greeted me with a long look and a smile. Jimmy Muro's (the steady cam man) reaction, I think was the best. I spoke to him as he hurried by. As he past me and picked up his camera it must have clicked on who I was. He looked up at me and didn't speak for a moment, just giving me that "I can't believe it's you look" with big eyes. He asked how I was and it was back to work. We weren't in for very long. Sit around a while and then we go back up on deck about 2:45 a.m. We are instructed to mill around on A Deck. Wandering around, trying to figure out how to put our life jackets on, I am with Brian and he is helping me. Then watching a lifeboat being lowered, really doubting that any problem exists and basically ignoring all warnings from the crew.

It is really weird watching the lifeboat being lowered. They really are lowering it with the big thick ropes, but there is a safety cable that runs down the sides of the ropes on each end of the boat that will engage if something were to slip. The cables then run through the ceiling of the Boat Deck, down into the wall of A Deck, where they are attached to five ton electric wenches that bring the boat back up to the Boat Deck again. This can be very time consuming. Those of us that are not on the boat go and get refreshments for our stranded friends and smuggle it to them as they go by. Our efforts are much appreciated. I finally get to see Kathy Bates, but don't have the chance to meet her. Everyone that has been able to meet her says she is fun. We wrap at 6:30 a.m.

December 13, Friday. Back to the set at 3:30 p.m. I dress 1st Class again. Up on the Boat Deck tonight. We are in a group that is trying to get to the lifeboats on the starboard side. I stop behind one of the davits and act like I can't get through. I am told to do my best not to be recognized. So I do a lot of gasping with my hands to my face or ducking behind the davit. The fear level is starting to increase now, as we begin to realize that the ship is actually going to sink. There is more crying and screaming for each other.

After awhile, Deena and I move over against the wall of the 1st Class gym. We stand there, talk, watch and wait. Then we make our way down to the holding area for a snack or something. Kari is looking for me. She tells me that my husband called and I have to call him back right away. So I go back down to casting and find out that I need to get home, because of my dad. Everyone is concerned and tells me to drive safe. I leave at mid-night. Home by 2:30 a.m. All has calmed down and my dad is fine. I call the set the next day and find out I'm not needed until Monday.

38

December 16, Monday

I get back down to the set at 4 p.m. Over the weekend I was able to make my pumpkin breads and I have made enough for the people that head up wardrobe, hair, make-up, casting and the guys at the gate. I also drop by the office and leave some for Mr. Landau, Josh, and Sebastian. I later deliver some for Mr. Cameron to his motor home.

I've been demoted to 3rd Class again. I have a different look tonight. A combo outfit, my dark blue, flowered shirt from the water scenes and my brown skirt I wore on the Poop Deck. We are inside tonight, on the Grand Staircase. We sit for awhile and I see this lady there. She is knitting something. I asked her what it was. She held it up proudly and showed me it was a baby blanket. She was making it for her sister that was due any day. As we visit, I learn that she is Suzy Amus, she plays the Granddaughter to "old Rose", Gloria Stuart's character. Sebastian calls and takes me over and places me where I will appear to be running out of the hallway near the elevators and out a side door onto the Promenade Deck. I am to be struggling with my life jacket as I run past Kate and

Leo, while Billy is shooting at them. As he tells me this, he thinks I might be too recognizable and I tell him that this is not my usual outfit tonight. Mr. Cameron is back by the monitors. He hears me tell Sebastian this and asks me how different this outfit is. When I tell him he says, "that will be even better," and has me stay. In between shots, Mr. Cameron asks me how the catering has been. I told him it is really bad. He kind of shook his head and said he wished he could do something about it, and I said "So do I." I told him that his pumpkin bread was waiting for him at the motor home. He said "Great" and then it was back to running. Kate and Leo pass me as I fling the life jacket up and over my head. I get out the door just as Billy is coming by.

After break, we go back up to the ship again. It's a nice night out, but it is a little cold. Sitting in the holding area is boring so I venture out to the Boat Deck to see what they are shooting now. They have been doing the scene when the ice falls on the forward Well Deck as the ship scrapes the berg. Kate and Leo are down there and so are a couple of stuntmen. I get to see them shoot this twice. There is a tower with a large tray and chute on it. Big chunks of ice are on the tray, which is tipped at an angle so the ice will slide down the chute on to the deck and anyone in the way. When action starts, Kate and Leo are startled by the impact of the ship against the berg, they watch in terror as the ice slams down on the deck, almost crushing the crewmen. On the last take, the man that releases the ice has a big red broom that he is using to push the ice down the chute. Well, this time the broom gets stuck and is pulled from the man's hands and comes down with the ice. This is the shot that Mr. Cameron likes the best, so I'm sure the big red broom won't spoil the shot, you won't know the entertainment that provided us tonight. Starting to feel the dampness & cold, now. We get wrapped at 5 a.m.

39

December 17, Tuesday

Wake up to the worst wind storm I've seen in a long time. Thank God, we are not working the Poop Deck anymore. This will definitely wreak havoc on the set tonight.

I get to the set and they tell me that they tried to call me, to tell me not to work, because they changed the shooting schedule. So I only get half pay, great…I really didn't need that to happen. The wind has torn down most of the tents that are around the studio. The only thing that is left of some of them are their steel skeletons. Catering has moved inside the wardrobe building. As we sit around and play games, the wind is raging. The lifeboats up on the ship had to be lowered onto the deck and tied down. A lot of damage is happening out there that no one can do anything about. It is so bad that a huge Quonset hut has blown over and moved across one of the lots to the other side of the street. They have a very unique way of stopping it, too. They took a concrete divider, like the kind used on the freeways, and dropped it in the middle of it. Oh well, it was ruined anyway. At least it didn't go anywhere after that.

Living the Legend: The Journal of a Titanic Background Actress

As we are waiting around I help Bo wrap and pack some Christmas presents for her family back East. We walk back and forth to the set a few times. They are shooting the inside Poop Deck. Ellen is standing in for one of the actresses again. This set is just the last 15 or 20 feet of the deck. It is on hydraulics and tilts just like the big one did. Kate and Leo are struggling to hold on as they climb over the rail and get ready for the stern's final plunge. The stunt crew is there and they help one of our kids slide down the deck into Simon Crane's waiting arms. They are shooting a lot of different angles and people, so this takes a long time. As we are sitting around, Mr. Landau, thanks me for his bread. He tells me that it was very good. I see Sebastian and he says the same thing. During a break, Mr. Cameron hurries by and sees me sitting with some of my friends. He says, "Hi" as he passes. On his way back he says "Thanks for the bread, Jude, it was great!" I told him he was welcome, as he hurried back to filming.

While we are sitting there, we are talking about the rumors that have gone around the set. Of course, none of them are very nice, mostly things about who is sleeping with whom and who is on drugs. So, as the brilliant minds of Ellen, Suzanne and I ponder on these things, we decide to make up our own tale. Tomorrow night we will start telling everyone that, while we were on the set last night, this is what we saw: We saw Josh get fired last night, because he laughed at something that happened to Mr. Cameron. Cameron was in the middle of a take and got mad. He ripped his earphones off (which many of us have seen numerous times) and his fake ear came off with them and fell on the floor. Ellen reached down to pick it up, but someone stepped on it and mashed it. Josh was hysterically laughing. Cameron, up-set with the whole event, fires Josh for laughing at him. Ellen then hands the ear to Cameron, he sees that it is ruined and tells her to keep it. Later, after he calmed down he signed it for her. Now, since Ellen makes prosthetics, she just happens to have an ear. She is to bring it to the set as proof of our dubious tale. Happy with what we have cooked up, we agree on all details and will launch it on our unsuspecting group tomorrow.

We sit around awhile longer. I am waiting for Ellen to get off, so I can take her to the hotel, her car won't start. It's really getting late and it looks as if she will have to stay for sometime, so I leave at 5:15 a.m.

40

December 18, Wednesday

Get up early, 2 p.m. and I go up to Ellen's hotel. We go out to see if we can start the car. Wade is there, we all stand there looking at the car and agree that a simple jump won't do it. It must be something electrical. We get to the set at 4 p.m. and find out there is no work, but to stick around and things might change. It is windy again, so we are still inside, so that means they are either working with crewmen or special shots with a small group. We are just sitting around, so we begin to tell our tale. Everyone is eating this up. Especially one of the gals in the office. She was getting ready to call someone up at the main office to see if Josh was coming back! We had her convinced that this was why we weren't doing anything tonight. We had to take her aside and tell her that it wasn't true. She was really a good sport about it and even sought out her own victims to tell. Unfortunately, Ellen didn't have the ear and couldn't get it until after Christmas break, but even without it, people were eating the tale up. We timed it. Only 20 minutes from one end of casting to the other. One of our friends took it so seriously that he sat there and proclaimed "You know, you can tell if you really look at Cameron closely that he wears a fake ear!" Since someone has now seen Josh on set, they think Mr. C isn't upset anymore and that it was just a spur of the moment outburst. So, we act accordingly and agree. We take pride in our accomplishment and just smile at each other. Our Titanic tale was a success!

I have more people sign my journal, I play Trivial Pursuit and take more pictures of all of us goofing around. Still no work at 11p.m. I say all my good-byes and Merry Christmas to everyone that I can. As I'm leaving I see Josh sitting during a break, they had moved their catering into where the "cement pond" was. I walk over and he thanks me for his bread and wanted to know how I found the time. I told him that I got to go home for a couple of days and that's when I made it all. We talk a little bit and I told him that I hope that he gets some good rest over break and that he gets his voice back. We wish each other Merry Christmas and I leave. I see some other crew people and leave at 11:30. Home and to bed by 2:15 a.m. It's the 19th so I am home for my dad's birthday. I probably won't work until Jan. 12th or 13th. They are going to shoot the flooding of the Grand Staircase tomorrow or the next day and then they get to break. I wish we could stay to see it, but it will be a closed set, because of the danger involved with the amount of water that will be dumped on the set. The construction crew gets to tilt the ship to 6½-7 degrees. That will look incredible.

41

January 13, 1997, Monday

It's been 3½ weeks. I wonder what's going on down at the set. Get a call to be on the set by 8:45 a.m. on Tuesday the 14th. I ask how things are going and I'm told just fine. I arrive at 8:30 and they tell me at the gate that the call time has been pushed back to 11 a.m. So, I go down to the house and unload all my stuff and get back to the set at 10:45. The ship looks incredible, at a 7° tilt, we will now start shooting the sinking scenes. A lot of deck work and long nights lay ahead of us now. At least that's what we think.

We don't get dressed until noon. We all sit around and talk about what we did while we were at home and celebrating the holidays with our families. We sit around and start playing Outburst. Suzanne and I kick butt. We still have not gotten called to the set. We did not get our New Year's wish either. We wanted new catering but, no such luck. After some salty "whatever it was" for dinner, we finally get called up to the set around 9 or 9:30 p.m. We are to be shadows seen through the stained glass windows of the Smoking Room that was built in one of the sound stages. This is fun, we keep running in a loop and doing different things. One time we got to scream and yell. The shoes that I'm wearing are like two clamps left over from the Spanish Inquisition, I have callous upon callous. I have bandages on four toes, two on each foot and one on each heel. Some times the pain is excruciating. I ask Lou, (he is a new assistant director that has just recently joined us), if I can take them off. A lot of us have our tennis shoes and they let us change when our feet can't be seen. He lets us do that, but cautions us that we will have to put them back on as soon as we go to the next set. As we start getting into what we are doing, I try to organize us into doing a little skit as we pass the windows. We all want to "walk like an Egyptian" but we don't want to do it if the camera is rolling. We end up doing this only in our imaginations, because we don't want to get killed! Boy that would have been hilarious though, if there had only been time. Everything is so rushed now.

Then we go over to the other inside set, just across the room. It is the exterior deck that passes by the Garden Room. We can be seen through these windows. Ellen and I do a few takes as if we get separated and she catches up. We grab each others' hands and run toward the stern. Then Rick & Lou tell me to run into the arms of Achilles, as Sebastian sends him back through the crowd. We are to act like we just found each other. I literally jump into his arms and he picks me up and twirls me around, then we proceed on our way to the stern. We do that a few more times. I can see Sebastian laugh every time we do this. It is starting to get hot again, but not nearly as bad as the Common Room. As I pass Sebastian, I ask him how many more times we are going to do this? He just smiles, and says " 'till we're done." Just a couple more takes and we wrap at about 4 a.m.

42

January 15, Wednesday

To the set at 3:30 p.m. We sit around up in the holding area of the ship and watch it start to rain. It's cold and the decks are not waterproof. Our area leaks, like a sieve. They must be shooting 1st Class stuff, because we in 3rd Class are all left to wait. We go down to dinner about 11 p.m. It really starts coming down hard now. We will stay in the wardrobe building the rest of the night. A couple of us sit down to play Trivial Pursuit. We just get a good game going and they tell us that we are all wrapped. Go home 12:30 a.m. I can sleep in!

January 16, Thursday. On set at 2:30 p.m. I get to dress 1st Class tonight. We are on deck by sunset. Peggy Pickard and I are put together up on the Observation Deck. We are up on the rail that is closest to the Forward 1st Class staircase entrance. We are listening to the band that has chosen to play there. We can see the commotion that is going on up by one of the lifeboats. Kate is trying to get away from Billy. She struggles to pull from his hold on her. She has to spit in his face, for real. She has to do this at least a dozen times. I hear Mr. Cameron ask if she has run out of spit yet. One of the make-up ladies has a bowl with egg whites. If Kate does run out of spit she will have to put those in her mouth to spit on Billy. All I can think of is it will make her puke if she has to hold those egg whites in her mouth, yuck. We are to watch and just be background. As we visit, we find out that we know a lot of old horse people in San Diego. We have a good time reminiscing about the shows and horses we knew. Now it starts to get cold and windy. I brought my big down filled jacket and we are able to wrap up in it between takes. I have my two layers of long underwear and I'm still cold. After break, we shift positions and are able to walk around, but basically we are doing the same thing as earlier.

During a break in what we were doing, I became bored and started one of my many exploration tours of the ship. I notice that Ed Marsh and Anders Falk have set up their camera next to a lone chair and a set of lights. Always enjoying any conversation I have with these two, I wander down the deck to see what they are doing. They are waiting for Frances Fisher to come over to give them an interview. While they are waiting, they are trying to get the light at the right angle so when she does come over she won't have to wait to long. I ask them if I could "stand in" for her until she arrived. They were very glad that I did, so they could set the lighting. During that time, Ed gives me an interview, too. It was fun the way they did it. Just like I was really somebody. They asked me what had been the most impressionable thing that I had done since I had been there. Hands down, it was the scene when lifeboat 14 comes back for survivors. I think the whole thing took about 5 minutes and then I had to get back. It sure helped the long night pass and I wondered what that interview might have looked like, Ed and Anders are great guys. We finally wrap at dawn.

43

January 17, Friday

To the set at 3 p.m. 1st Class again, now up to the Promenade Deck on the ocean side of the ship. This deck is the nicest to be on because it is enclosed, so we are able to keep warm. We are to provide bodies moving up and down this deck as they are lowering the lifeboat with Kathy Bates. After accomplishing this task, Ellen, Marshal (Jon Landau's Father-in-law) and I are laying around on deck chairs. As the boat gets lowered to our level, we see a bunch of our friends sitting in it, and the show begins. On the first take we all make faces at them. This provoked them to do the same. Now we get creative, Marshal says "Let's moon them!" So we do, with our clothes on though. Marshal flipped up the tails on his tux, and all they get of us is our ugly slips. We must be careful to make sure that Josh has hollered "cut" before we begin our shows. Things are cooking now. Next we do the Can-Can, we can see that we are killing them. We can hear Josh telling them to quit laughing! Now we perform the Macaraina. We can see them trying to ignore us but, they can't. Then Ellen and Marshal leave for awhile. At this point, the FX guys that are raising and lowering the lifeboat are just inside the windows behind us on the Promenade. They have been trying to watch our little shows, but haven't been able to see everything. So we goof around with them, too. We go to the window and act like they are a fast food place, ordering the kind of food that we can only dream of down here. In the meantime, Ralph has been on the floor asleep during all of this and he wakes up. So I recruit him and we talk to each other, ignoring those in the boat. They tap on the glass and try to get our attention but to no avail. This provokes them into flipping us off. Now we act like we are asleep. We can hear them tapping again. Ellen returns and we discuss our next course of action. Well, Robert comes along just in time for the next performance and I call him over and told him to make love to me. Before I could explain what we were doing and that we had to wait for "cut", he jumps on top of me. Now you must visualize this. I am sitting in a lounge chair, with my feet up. His legs are on the <u>outside</u> of mine and he is bending over me. I start kicking my legs like I'm swimming and pulling up the back of his shirt. I guess it gave a good effect, everyone was laughing hysterically. We hear another command to keep quiet, and they wrote a note saying that Cameron was on his way down to see what was going on. That was our last performance, they had finished, so the show was over. We received rave reviews from our fellow background actors that night. No, Mr. Cameron never came down. So now it's back up to the Boat Deck for more walking around until dawn.

44

January 18, Saturday

Back to the set at 3:30 p.m. 1st Class again, I kind of miss my 3rd Class though. Tonight we get to be in lifeboat 12 as it is being lowered. This is thrilling and scary too. We end up having a great time. Joey, from stunts and also double for Leo, is with us, so is Eunice, she is a stunt woman that had a black eye from the Poop Deck shots. I asked her what had happened, she told me that she fell on someone's knee and it had shattered her cheek bone. She was really lucky that it didn't puncture her eye. As they are lowering the boat, they can't get it to go down straight. We would get so far and one end would go down farther then the other, thus causing a few anxious moments for thrill sake. It felt weird when they would let the boat down, because it would jerk and shake. I don't know how many times we went up and down. A couple of times we got all the way to the water. They would actually lower us by hand, with that two inch thick rope. Later I find out that the block and tackle set up, is a six to one ratio, which means for every six turns we went down one foot. Putting that into perspective for that night so long ago, just think how hard and time consuming it was to get the boats to lower away. At one point, one of the A.D.s comes up and starts telling me to stop throwing things out of the lifeboat. I told him "it wasn't me. I would never do something stupid like that." Someone down below had accused me of hitting them with jelly beans and other things. Everyone in our boat knew it wasn't me and they all told him so. He called down and told Josh that it wasn't me doing it. He was told to find out who it was and make them stop! Not only that, I was on the inside of the boat, closest to the side of the ship, so even if I wanted to throw something out, I would not have been able to. That was really aggravating getting accused of something like that, it could have gotten me fired. Later, we find out it was actually one of the men doing it.

After dinner, we walk the decks. We are to be a little more rushed and panic is starting to set in as the life boats begin to fill and leave. It's cold and we huddle together when and where ever we can. I have my Tasmanian Devil ear muffs and am the envy of all. Doug, the camera grip, has a funny hat, too. We call him Nanuk. We both wear our WARM hats with pride. Everyone else is just jealous. We have a Kodak moment to commemorate our bravery and distinction. We wrap at 6 a.m. and I head for home. Spend Sunday, where else? At the movies seeing "The Relic", pretty good. Go home and sleep.

45

January 20, Monday

Back down to the set at 4 p.m. Dress 3rd Class tonight and do a lot more running around on the Promenade Deck. We are to provide the "frenzied" look. In between takes we play musical deck chairs in hopes of sitting down. It's cold, but we are having fun running into each other. Dinner? Hardly! I've started to bring my own food again. We go back up on deck and do more of the same until dawn. Don't get to bed until 7:30 a.m. though. The way the sun rises in the east makes it really hard to see when you are traveling south. So if you don't get on the road before 7 it can be dangerous. I just wait until the sun is a little higher in the sky. I sit and have some pancakes with Zubie, who has just gotten to work. He asks how the night went and I told him about the lifeboat scenes.

January 21, Tuesday. Back again at 3 p.m. Same thing as the night before. We have Lou as our assistant director, again. He is always fun to work with. He's cute too, reminds you of the Marlboro man. He puts us into different groups and has us do different things. After break, they get us into lifeboats again. Sometimes we can be in them for several hours. It can be fun out there, but I'm glad to be where I'm at. I'm able to move around and stay warm. We run goodies to those that we can reach, i.e. cokes, chips, candy, you know, basic junk. Apples and grapes are popular, too.

Kate is supposed to jump out of collapsible D onto the Promenade Deck. As we are running by, we see her and act like we can't believe what she is doing. Two men that are passing, see that she is struggling to get back on board and assist her. We seem to get a lot done, but who knows. Boy, do my feet hurt. I sit every chance I get. We wrap at 5:30, to bed by 7 a.m.

46

January 22, Wednesday

We get to the set a little earlier today, 2:30 p.m. More of the same. Watching them lower the boats, panic, general mangling of our bodies, the usual. We do have fun tonight, things are moving right along. It's too bad every night can't be like this. I'm sure Mr. Cameron feels the same way. Oh well, we are a work in progress, what more can I say?

It is really cool how they have illuminated the decks. They have 1 x 3 inch boards with 100 watt light bulbs sticking up through holes that they have drilled in them. They are laying next to the rails the entire length of the deck. People keep kicking them and of course they break. We are supposed to look over the rails occasionally to see what is going on below. In so doing we have to get next to the lights. Sometimes our skirts touch them and get burned. Ellen's skirt burned clear through one night. Stunts add to the problem as well. They have them up on the Boat Deck, right above us, falling into the water. So every time the stunt crew comes back up they are wet & the water drips through the deck planks down on us. Well, water and electricity don't mix. All we can do is watch the drama unfold. The water is cold and drips down on the hot lights so they pop. The lighting guy thinks we kicked them. He comes out, all bent out of shape at us, mumbling how stupid we are. I explain to him the situation and his attitude changes. Now, there are those that no matter how many times you warn or explain a situation, they just don't listen or understand, they are just plain dumber then dirt. This was not one of those cases and I was glad to say so. I have gotten tired of hearing things about us from people that don't like "extras" that act like we really are cattle and talk down to us. Some of us have better educations then they do, just not the pay checks and they are just snotty and mean. Glad there are only about five of those people around and that we don't have to deal with them much.

Things change a little now and we move up and down the deck more. At one point, we head up the stairs to the Boat Deck. This staircase can only handle single file lines. When I got to the top, there was a big group of people pushing and I do mean pushing, towards the lifeboat. I got pushed into the back of a guy that was jumping up and down. Well, he landed on me, right on the top of my left foot. It was instant pain and I had to go down and sit out a couple of takes. As we sat there, just below the Wheel House, we could hear the "panic" of the crowd when cameras rolled. It gave a whole different feeling just listening to what we were doing. Now, still functional, I go back to "up and down" the Promenade Deck. Lou has me run against a crowd of people that are coming up the deck in the opposite direction. I do this about six times. I ask Lou why they always have me do these weird things. He responds, as he is moving away quickly and with a devilish grin, "Because you're lively!" I said "Thanks!" Smiling, I proudly go do my thing. Wrap at 5:30 a.m. I examine my injury and chalk it up to experience. Just black and blue, it could have been worse. Off to sleep.

47

January 23, Thursday

To the set at 3:30 p.m. Call home, all is well. Up on deck ASAP. They want to get rolling right away. I'm with a group of people that is pushing forward to Boat 14. Two stunt people are up front. A stuntman that I don't know and stuntwoman named Si. As we push, he knocks her over the edge, we respond by trying to get her back up, but someone on the lower deck grabs her and pulls her back on deck. During one take the stuntman could not hear "cut", a couple of us in the rear could and stopped pushing. We tried to stop those in front of us, but they either didn't understand or they didn't believe us. They kept reacting to what the stuntman was doing and Si almost fell. We were about 60 feet above water level and she was dangling, bare hands on a half inch steel lip on the edge of the deck. It was very intense, Cameron and Josh were screaming "cut, cut, cut, damn it cut!" A lot of the problem again, was with the people that hadn't been there before and were acting like stupid showoffs. Mr. Cameron was in the tower crane basket, if he could have reached them, he would have had their hides and we would have helped. After a long, angry lecture, we do it some more. Mr. Cameron then lands his basket on deck. As he sees me, he puts his hand on my shoulder and greets me again. He is very aware of who does what.

After break, we do more crowd stuff. Josh asks me to run from the rail of the Promenade that is over looking the rear Well Deck, to the rail just aft of Boat 14 and then down to the side of Boat 14. That is when I join the crowd scene that we shot earlier. Just before dawn, we do a reverse shot of the pushing crowd. Second Officer Lightoller, has a gun that he threatens us with. It is empty, as he points it at us and says "I'll shot you like dogs!" He then turns away, and loads it. We stay until 7 a.m. for this shot. We wrap just as the light starts to change as the sun comes up. Finally to bed by 9 a.m.

48

January 24, Friday

Get to come in a little later tonight, 4:30. We had some rain and the parking lot is a stinking mess again. Dirty tennis shoes and all, I get to wardrobe and up on deck by 6, just sitting around doing nothing. I guess a lot of stunt work is going on. We hear rumors that we might not work tomorrow, but won't know for sure until later. Break for dinner, crap again, so what's new? Back to the ship and find a warm spot, glad I have an extra shirt. I rolled it up and wrapped it around my neck. Signed up for a premiere party that Eileen is talking about. She works at the Hotel Del Coronado, sounds like it will be fun. As I retreat to the catering area, looking for something warm to consume, I find one of the hair dressers and visit. As we are standing there, we see one of the actresses walk in. I know I have seen her in things before, but can't place her. She walks over and talks with us. She tells us some of the things that she has appeared in Colombo, Murder She Wrote, Matlock & Diagnosis Murder, Star Trek Next Generation just to name a few. She was in Mr. Cameron's first film, her name is Tricia

O'Neil, a very nice, stunning lady. She talked with us for quite sometime. She was taking a break, because she had fallen during the filming of one of her scenes. She said she had just skinned her shins a bit while getting in or out of the lifeboat. She got her scuba license when she did "Piranha" and has been friends with Cameron ever since. She called him and asked for a job on this film and he gave her this part. She signs my journal and tells me to try to get on T3! I thanked her and she went back up to where she came from.

Still just sitting around. It's colder tonight, two more hours to go. I guess we feel the cold more because we aren't moving around very much. Do nothing and wrap at 6 a.m. No work tomorrow, so I go home.

49

January 27, Monday

Just had two days off and it's back to the set at 3 p.m. It starts off kind of boring. We are on B Deck, it is just a little tiny hallway that doesn't go anywhere. It is not finished, very little lighting, we are on a gang way used to access the electrical for the ship. When action is called, we emerge as if we are coming up from below decks. It is very cold tonight, I go down at break and put more clothes on. Come back up and do different things on the same deck. I have to run out a door, up the deck a bit, turn around and go back as if I have forgotten someone or something.

Later, Mr. Cameron gets in his really cool helicopter. He has a nose camera and goes around the ship a few times as Josh coordinates us. We are to look like we are at a 45° angle when action starts. We all do this very well, so we only have to do this about three times. We wrap at 6 a.m. and I take Bo back to her place with the things I brought from Price Club for her dogs when I went home over the weekend. To bed by 8:30.

January 28, Tuesday. To the set at 3:30 p.m. Dress for 3rd and ready to be in the prayer group again. We meet up with James Lancaster (Father Byles), Linda Kern and Brian Walsh (from the Gaelic Storm band in 3rd Class). In between takes, I get them all to sign my journal. We have a good time running around and laughing at Lucy and Nikki beating up on each other. Everytime we are in "action" these two act like they are fighting for deck space. We do this about seven times. Then we move to the Boat Deck. We are to do deep background movement for the scenes that they are shooting on the other side. This means that we won't be seen at all. So while we wait, we eat nachos and any other junk that sounds appealing at the moment. We have our own deck picnic. It's cold tonight, but not like it was the night before, we still huddle to keep warm.

Now it's back to the Well Deck for the panic shots. Joy. We must give the impression of mass panic, running up the stairs. These scenes are very hard to control. Way too many first timers again, that don't care about those around them. They are jumping on people, stepping on each other, some getting hurt because of careless individuals. The AD's keep telling them to be careful, but they don't listen. It gets so bad that I move to the outer edge to keep from getting hurt. I find Bo off to one side and just watch a couple of takes. It was sheer mayhem. The big guys just run right over you. One girl leaves in tears, saying some one felt her where she shouldn't have been felt, she said it felt like they were holding her down on purpose and molesting her. The men that were in the area of that shot are reprimanded, being told that if the individual was found, that he would be brought up on assault charges. This type of activity will not be tolerated. Don't know if it happened to anyone else. I hope not. I felt so sorry for this girl.

While we are waiting around, Sebastian calls me over to the rail to be in camera for about two seconds. Mr. Cameron is in the tower crane basket right in front of me. I watch the stunt people jump over the side, then run to the stairs as Kate and Leo are running from C Deck to the Well Deck. We are all headed to the stern.

After break, we go back for more crowd "crush and run" scenes for the remaining 4½ hours. It's rough on all of us. No one can control the out of control idiots that are around us. All of us regulars are furious, but helpless to make it stop. Glad to wrap at 6:30.

50

January 29, Wednesday

Back to the set again at 4 p.m. Up on the Boat Deck again. We are just wandering quickly around. Marcia and her daughter are here tonight for the lifeboat scenes. We watch Billy Zane and the dogs run up the deck past us. It appears that Billy is looking for a lifeboat to get into.

As we are watching, we see Bill Paxton come on deck. He sit's at the video village and watches the action. He looks thinner then he did in "Twister" and of course all of us women think he's cute. He is totally taken with the set. He can't believe how real everything and everyone looks. He acts like a little kid that has just found a cave to explore. We break for dinner. Crap again and even hear that about 70 people got sick from the night before, but who knows.

We are summoned to the stern and reassemble the prayer group again. It is windy and we are up there for a while before they move the cameras and equipment back here. As we sit in groups on the deck, we can feel the structure sway in the wind. You see, the Poop Deck is on a huge scaffolding structure. Because of the 7° angle that the ship is tilted to, it is also very high up. The rest of the ship, from the Well Deck forward is on a much larger and firmer "I" beam frame work. It is a visual thing as well. The scaffolding looks like tooth picks compared to the rest. I sure don't like it up here. The wind is blowing harder now. Sitting still doesn't help keep my mind off of it. I start feeling panicky, like I have to get off…get off now! I told Sebastian that I had to get down and relax for a minute. I went and got a drink and when I came back he let me stand closer to the Well Deck where the motion wasn't as bad. That helped a lot, I have never felt like that before. It is strange how I love roller coasters, and didn't mind the Poop Deck at all when it was down on the lift. But, I will not go up in a tall building and look down or go to the very end of the Poop Deck to do the same. Just sitting here writing this…my hands are sweaty.

They finally start setting up on the Poop Deck. Bill Paxton comes back to watch. As Mr. Cameron tells where he wants his video village, Bill starts talking to all of us. The make-up ladies have taken some of us aside and put tears on us again. But, just before they get to me, Barbarela asks to take a picture with Bill. I get in it too, and he puts his arms around us for the shot. He tells us how impressed he is with the set and how great we all look. He tells us how exciting it is to be a part of this and what it was like for him on "Apollo 13", replaying history is a great experience for anyone. Later he signs my journal! After we finish with the prayer group, I move down to the Well Deck. While we were moving around and doing the takes, I didn't notice the motion. I guess my mind was occupied, so I didn't think about it at all.

We are on stand by as they try to set the shot before the sun comes up. All we can do is watch what the crew is doing. They are working with the stunt crew again. It has been a hard night for all the crew. At one point, I found Bo in tears and Mr. Cameron was not a whole lot of happy with Josh. Things aren't going well. Finally they wrap us at 6:15 a.m. I'm told that I am a primary extra (which is a fancy name for someone they have on set all the time), which I already knew. Oh well, I'm here all the time and I will work to the end. Loving it!

🙞 51 🙜

January 30, Thursday

Arrive on set at 4 p.m. Up on deck by 5:30 and told to report to Rick downstairs. We are in a little group that is to look like we are crowding the 3rd Class entrance gang way door on the lower level. We are trying to get to the lifeboats. Danny Nucci is down there with us. He is really a nice guy, but he smokes these horrible smelling cigars all the time. He is really proud of his new baby girl that was born back in October. So he has no problem telling us how his wife and daughter are doing. We are down here for about three hours. It really is boring, because we can't see anything. It's funny, there are only two of us that are short. We are right in the middle of the group. We can't see out and no one can see us. So from the outside it looks like there is a big hole in the middle of the group unless we put up our hands.

Finally, after our exile, we are brought back up on top again. We watch the lifeboats being lowered. They are filming when Boats 13 & 15 almost collide when they are being lowered. As 15 is actually lowered onto 13. During this action we do more of our running "back and forth panic" routine. I stop for a moment and watch what happens with the boats. It is very intense. Reality is what they are after and it comes pretty dang close. Everything has to be exact or 15 will hit 13. During one take it is so real that the people inside the boats actually convince the crew to stop lowering the boats! They really thought something was wrong. Great acting!!

After break, we gather on board and do nothing. We have to wait for the shots to be set. Background panic again, but that is few and far between. They are working on the deck by Collapsible C. Mostly with stunt people I guess. Bo has me go down there, but Josh can't use me and sends me back. I watch a little of what is being done. Jay is in the lifeboat and he is supposed to cut a rope on queue. During the take Mr. Cameron is in the boat with his shoulder camera. I guess he wanted to film the rope being cut. I don't know exactly what happened, but the next thing I hear is "cut, cut!" and Jay is cutting the rope as fast as he can, but the "cut" that was being yelled, was meant to stop action. Jay was totally confused and cut the rope. Thus causing Mr. Cameron extreme displeasure and he was very angry with Jay. Jay probably wanted to crawl away and die. I had only seen Mr. Cameron upset like that on four other occasions, when it cost him a shot and when someone almost got hurt. We all get quiet and don't say a word. Not too sure what happened after that. I went back to holding and do what we always do, talk and eat until we wrap at 6:30 a.m.

January 31, Friday. Back to the set at 4 again. We hurry to get dressed and get up on deck by 5:30. Damn we are good! We do more of our favorite thing, running up and down like chickens with our heads cut off. We then stop and sit around doing our next favorite thing which is nothing, talking and eating. I swear I don't know where we put all this junk. We break for dinner, hoorf! Go back up on deck to do nothing again. About 4:30 a group of us gets pulled to go with Josh. He tells us to run up the deck, past the band that is playing just outside the 1st Class Boat Deck entrance. We are to be looking back at the water that is rushing up the deck. We get to do this a couple of times. Then the fog rolls in, heavy, it's so thick, we can't even see the forth funnel as we look up the deck from the Boat House. So we wrap at 5:15 a.m. Wouldn't you know that by the time I get out of wardrobe at 6 the sky is clear. Great, to bed early!

52

February 1, Saturday

Since we left early last night, we have to come back at 3 p.m. today. Up on deck to do the same scene that we ended with last night. They are ready to roll at 5:30, this is one of the fastest start ups since the "cement pond." It's going to be a long night. We are to run up from the 1st Class Lounge, where the band is, round the Observation Deck, between the 2nd and 3rd funnels, to the other side of the Observation Deck and up the Observation Deck stairs. Next, it's down that deck to the Compass Tower, run under it, then to the stairs that lead down near the band and back up the deck again. A big circle of panic best describes it. The first take is long, we make it around three times. Just before the forth lap, Cameron yells "cut". We all breathe a sigh of relief. You can hear a collective laughter from one end of the ship to the other. We thought he was going to go for a record on the next shot. Mr. Cameron must have felt sorry for us, because the next takes were not that long. But, it does get rough. Brad, Mary and I are to run out first. On "action" we go. We are to try to warn the band that the water is coming up fast. As we run, we keep looking behind us, so those that are coming down the deck in the opposite direction, are to watch out for us. They can see us before we see them. These people are doing something different then we are. One guy is supposed to run down and fall next to the band. The first two takes go ok. On the 3rd, things go wrong. This time we cross paths and I don't see him soon enough to avoid a collision, but he does see me and doesn't move to the side. He deliberately plants himself, like a football player, and hits me in the chest with his shoulder. This forces me backwards and I could feel my back almost give out. I swing my arm to keep my balance and asked what he thought he was doing as we keep going, but I'm pissed and hurt. As I run up the deck, I see him sitting on the deck near Bo. I go over to him and tell him that he better not hit me like that again. He doesn't speak much English, but he knew what he had done and what I was telling him. I told Bo briefly as I continued on my way. As I go, some of the electricians and stunt people had picked up on what had happened and asked me about it. They said they would watch out for the guy and that he better not do it again. I'm sore, but we must go again. This time he hits Mary and Brad. On the way up, Bo says she has taken care of him. I told her that this time he hit two other people in front of me. Sebastian gets involved and stops him from running down the deck at us. We could see Sebastian talking to him and he was glaring and I do mean glaring at us as Sebastian was talking. So he decides to leave the spot where he was supposed to be now and come down to our group. He starts talking to his friends, little does he know that these guys are my friends too, and starts telling them in Spanish what had happened. We knew enough to know that he was trying to blame us for his carelessness. Josh was standing right there and hears me tell this guy that what had happened was his own fault and that he shouldn't be down here trying to start trouble. Josh stops me and asks what was going on and I begin to tell him, but by that time I was upset and talking too loud. Josh told me to calm down, that we didn't need this kind of thing going on. I could tell he was upset with me over my outburst. I apologize and we go again. Now, after each take, this guy stands where he can stare at us and give us dirty looks. He is making us feel like he is going to do something to us later. Well, by now a number of people know what is going on, because he is talking about us everywhere he goes. Little does he know, all the people he tells have been there longer and know us better, so he looks like the idiot. The special effects guys, electricians on deck, and the stuntmen are pissed off at him, because myself and a few others have been hurt by this guy and the other hot doggers that have been there this past week. They tell me that if it happens again they'll be there. Things continue on an even keel the rest of the night, but he follows Mary and I where ever we go. We stay together and with other people so he can't get behind us. At break he waits for us at one of the gates on deck. We see him and we try to ignore him, but he moves into out path, just looking at us. As we get close to him, he brushes my shoulder with his as I go through the gate. He then follows us down the stairs. He backs off when he sees Bruce talking to us. We tell Lou about him and Bo knows what he's up to now. They are watching him, along with about a dozen others. We have no problems at dinner or the rest of the night.

Back on deck, to a new scene. We are around Collapsible A. About eight of us women have to fight through a crowd to get to the boat. Billy Zane is with us in this shot. We had a nice conversation with him as we stand around waiting. I asked him where his part is in "Back to the Future", he is one of Biff's gang members. He was happy to speak with us, a really nice man. Don't think you'll see me in any of these shots, though. Billy is trying to get to the boat. The men were instructed not to be rough, but it doesn't do any good. The first take is fun, I mean really really fun. I ended up in a pile of stuntmen against the wall of the wheel house. These stuntmen picked me up like a rag doll by the shoulders and bounced me up and down! They made fun of how small I am and that they could do a lot with me. I asked them what they meant by that and they just laughed. Next, they push Collapsible A off the roof of the boat house and it crashed to the deck and we jumped out of the way. Things got a little rough and the crowd is cautioned again against pushing and shoving each other. On the third take, Josh starts yelling cut and the pushing doesn't stop. On the third or fourth "cut" I get pushed to the deck, bam! Right down in front of Mr. Cameron. He is holding his hand held camera. As he lowers it quickly, he starts yelling at the crowd. He says, "What the hell is wrong with you people? How many times do you have to be told not to push like that? I don't want to see any of my women hit the deck like that again!" He says "Josh, Sebastian, you tell them again in English and Spanish not to do that!!" Josh helps me up and Mr. Cameron held my arm and asks if I'm OK. I give a nod, yes and proclaim "I would only give up if I had broken something or needed stitches!" No worse for wear, we go again. It is still rough, but at least they stop on "cut." We wrap at 6:30 a.m. I find a great surprise when I get back to wardrobe. Amy had come and gotten my book to take it to Kate to sign. I could not believe what a nice message she wrote to me. Pleased with the end of the night, I lick my wounds, take some aspirin and die for the night!

53

February 3, Monday

Back to the set at 3 p.m. and up on deck by 5:30. We pick up from Saturday and things are not as bad. Mr. Cameron sees me and asks how I am. He says "You looked a little red faced after being roughed up like that the other night." I just kind of laugh and he hurries off to his duties. We get into Collapsible A and they rock the boat as we do our "fright show." The water is rushing up the deck and we are reacting to that and the hysterical people that are trying to get in the boat with us. On one take I accidentally scratch the lady next to me on her cheek. As I turn back, Maria pokes me right in the eye. What a night so far. We do our best to keep our acting going and it doesn't mess up any of the shot. After "cut", one of the stunt guys asks if we are OK. Memo says we did great and that is the take he likes the best, he says we are all good stunt women. They are also doing the shooting scene, where 1st Officer Murdock shoots Jason during the scuffle for the lifeboat. They had shot this earlier on the opposite side of the ship and they were using a lot of fake blood (Karo syrup, glycerin and red dye) and apparently it wasn't flowing properly, so they tried to do it again on this side. We continue with this scene until break.

After dinner, a new scene. We are to walk up and down the deck as the drunken cook throws a chair over the side. This is fun, because we are trying to ask the 1st Class passengers for help and they don't want to even get near us. So the first classers that I know, I tell them to go "eat their shorts, bite me," and anything else endearing that comes to mind and they do the same to us.

Now we move to Collapsible D, where Kate jumps out of it to get back on deck so she can rejoin Leo. On our way over to where we are going to shoot this scene, I see Kate and thank her for the note she wrote to me. She told my "you're welcome, I was glad to do it." I also see Amy and tell her what a surprise it was that she had done that for me. Now it is time to work on the Promenade Deck. As they are setting up the shot, I look up and notice that there is the fake blood coming through the upper deck from the previous blood bath upstairs. It has made its way through the planks and is now dripping from the "I" beam above on to the deck that we will be filming the next scene on. There really is a lot of it and it looks as if the ship is bleeding…kinda freaky. I let one of the guys from props know and they have to clean everything off so it doesn't show up on film. After some quick clean up we are ready to go. I am placed in Kate's path as she is running up the deck away from the lifeboat and we almost collide. Next they move me a little closer to the lifeboat and I am standing on the deck with Beline as Kate jumps back onto the deck. We do a few different shots until we wrap at 6:15 a.m.

February 4, Tuesday. To the set at 3:30 and up on deck by 5:30 p.m. We are deep background tonight. We all kind of play around and explore the ship. I see Wade up on the roof of the room in between the third and fourth funnels. I go up and join him. What a view! We explore as much as possible before they switch scenes and have us do something else. Before I get down I spot Ellen on the Compass Platform. That was really a great place to look around and hide between takes. I got a lot of exercise going up and down the stairs. We mess around until about 10:45. They start calling for all 3rd Class core off the ship and to go to the indoor set. I stay back and sit by the elevator. Then, Sebastian comes by and sees me sitting there and he asks me why I haven't gone down to the other set like he said to. I tell him, because I'm not core. He doesn't seem to believe me and says "Like hell you're not! Get in the elevator and go!" Yvette kids with me and says to get the hell back up there with the other extras. Sebastian says to Yvette "I want all primary core supplementals, of which Judy must be the president of (i.e. Regular Extras Association-REA) to go." He looks at me and says "Not core? I don't believe it. Why Not?" I say "I don't know, I have asked for it all along. I guess there just hasn't been a spot open." He says, "If anyone should be core, it should be you, that's bull, that there wasn't any spots open. They should have made you core the first month." I said "all it really meant was that I got paid if I didn't work all the time, so I'm here all the time anyway. I would rather be here for it all and that's what I am."

Now, off the ship and in the largest of buildings, we are on set 2, the Labyrinth! A mass of corridors on the inside of the ship, constructed just under the Dining Room. We are trying to find our way out. Josh gives safety instructions and cautions us that we can get lost if we don't pay attention. I find you can get lost even if you do pay attention. I was on one side of the set and emerged on the other, on my way to the restroom. There was no danger as long as we weren't working on the sinking set. That would come later. A lot of waiting around as Mr. Cameron switches direction and groups of 3rd Class.

Wow! The gift horse opened its mouth for awhile tonight. We got to eat at the real goodie table for about 15 min. I just don't get it, why there is such a difference between to two places. I know I have to quit bitching about it, because it isn't going to change, not this late in the game. So I vent with writing about it.

We are asked to make sure that we don't bother the actors too much (which we already know) and to caution those that haven't been around that long, if we see them bugging any of the actors. We do a few more takes and then wrap at 5:45.

54

February 5, Wednesday

It's to the set again at 3:30. We are in the labyrinth on the staircase. Josh tells me that he doesn't want to see me during the take, so I don't go where the camera can see me. Then after a few takes Sebastian takes some of us off. There is an actress there that is playing the Irish mommy with two small children. She looks very familiar. I keep staring at her trying to place where I have seen her. Then it clicks and she just happens to notice that I keep looking at her. I apologize, and say she looks familiar. Then I ask if she played Vesqes on "Aliens". She smiles and says "Yes, but can you believe that it's been 10 years since that film?" I tell her that her face is familiar, but the hair (redhead with freckles) and the accent (Irish) is throwing me off. She is very nice, and visits with us a while and tells of how she got hired by Mr. Cameron for this and the other films. Her name is Janet, but I can't remember her last name. Now it's back to work. We stand on the staircase and watch them film Janet's part about 3 times. She is telling the children that as soon as they get done with the 1st Class people, they will then get to us.

During break, we spot Tom Arnold at the goodie table. He says "Hello" to those of us he passes by. After that little distraction, we discuss how comfortable the set is. Not hot like we thought it was going to be. I guess everyone was dreading coming inside, because of how miserable the last inside set was. Now we go back in and Sebastian is in a funny mood. He is singing and laughing at different things. Now things really start heating up. I sneak away to go to the restroom and when I come back they are in the middle of the shot, so I can't go back to where I was. I stand to the side and just watch with Maria and some others. While we were there, someone on the stairs starts cutting these really raunchy farts, silent bombs. Everyone starts talking and groaning. Sebastian comes over to see what the ruckus is. We tell him and we all start laughing, especially when he tells everyone to control their bodies and that there will be no more beans served. That statement prompted a cheer. Now, Josh and Cameron are up stairs watching the monitors and they have no clue of what is happening downstairs with us. So, Josh calls down to Sebastian wanting to know what was going on and to keep us quiet. Sebastian starts explaining to Josh what the situation is and that starts us all laughing again. Maria, myself and the group we are with, are hysterical and got too loud and Sebastian has us move away to a side room down the hall. We go back up on the staircase a little later and shoot a couple more takes and then wrap at 6:15 a.m. This was one of our more entertaining nights.

February 6, Thursday. I don't have to be to the set until 4 today. We do a lot of sitting around tonight. The rats are being used or I should say they are being trained for their part tomorrow night. It is really interesting how they do it. The rats are in a box at one end of the hall and there is another box at the other end where they will get their goodies. They open the box that they are in and blow a whistle, they all run out and scurry to the other box, except for one. He did not want to cooperate. I watch the trainer try to encourage him with a broom. He still will not go. I ask what is wrong with him and she tells me that he is afraid of going in because yesterday another rat beat him up and he is associating that box with a bad experience. She finally has to pick him up and take him to where he is supposed to be. After watching that for awhile, we do some background stuff and a quick scene with Kate and Leo, just moving through the hallway. Get a quick greeting from Mr. Cameron again. Then we do more stairway action. We joke about the last time we were here, hoping we don't have a repeat of the night before. Back to sitting around, eat, talk, tell jokes, etc. Wrap some of us at 5:15.

55

February 7, Friday

I get up a little early and I try to listen to the news, but it is so windy outside that the satellite dish moves and it distorts the picture. So I put in "True Lies". As I am watching, it comes to the part where the two Harrier jets are flying toward the bridge. As the pilot speaks to Arnold, I realize the voice I am hearing belongs to James Cameron. I listen three times. No mistake, it is him. I must ask Jim Schmidt tonight if I get a chance if he knows if Mr. Cameron supplied that voice.

Now it is back to the set at 4 p.m. again. To the inside set we go. It is a bit windy tonight so it is much more comfortable being inside. As we are waiting around, we can hear the whistles for the rats being used. There a couple of places that we can stand and look down on everyone during filming, but we must be very quiet. If we are moving around, we have to stop when they call "action". Everything is plywood flooring that separates the decks of the set. When you have on hard soled shoes, it can be very loud when walking around.

While we are waiting, I am told to go find Sebastian because he is looking for me. I find him downstairs and he tells me to go to Josh. So I find Josh and he tells me to sit on the floor next to a door in the hallway. He tells me to be crying, hysterically and fighting those that want me to get up. So I give it my best shot and ask if that is what he is looking for. He just looks at me and doesn't say a word. He walks away and the other assistant that is standing there with me doesn't know what to think either. So we just look at each other and shrug our shoulders, like I don't know? Next thing I know is that Josh comes back with Maria and then Cameron comes out and tells what he is looking for. She does it perfect, she's Italian and it was just what he wanted. She gets the part and she really deserved it. She was awesome. They put a mic on her and everything. Oh, well I missed out on another one, but I am thrilled that I even got to try for it. I just wish Mr. Cameron had instructed me on what to do.

A few of us are told to go put on our Southampton clothes. We do and then we don't do anything. They wrap us at 4 a.m.

February 8, Saturday. Over sleep, late to the set at 4:30. Not a big deal, but I still don't like to do things like that. Off to the inside set, down in the corridors. The camera is set up in the middle of the hall on the little cart with wheels and a seat. Josh greets me with a big smile and asks how I am. Glad to see him smile again, things must be going well this evening. Mr. Cameron has me right next to him, just to the right of the camera lens. He wants me to be a focal point for a little girl that is hurrying through the hall with her family. She is to just keep looking at me. On "action", the grips have to pull Cameron backwards as we move forward. This should look really cool. Hans is a little ways back from me. He is carrying this big trunk and with him being so tall (at least 6'6") it makes him look even taller. Well, the joke is, now that I am 3rd Class again, that I have killed my rich cousin in 1st Class and stuffed her in that trunk! Hmm, another sequel "Murder on the Titanic"? We do this a few times and then are told to go change into our Poop Deck clothes.

Next, Kristie and I are asked to go get some wet suit booties, because we may be used for some water activities. It would be running up the hall with the rats in front of us and the water would only be up to our ankles. We eat and sit around. We only get to watch some of the activities below. Mr. Cameron decides that women probably were not in this area at this point of the sinking. What a bummer, it would have been just the two of us and 4 or 5 men, Wade being one of them and we now call him the "bare-chested rat runner" because he doesn't have a shirt at the first part of the scene. So, we just end up sitting around, hoping that Mr. Cameron might change his mind. He doesn't, so we wrap at 5:15.

February 10, Monday. Didn't get a call to come in, but hoping to get used anyway. I end up going to dinner with Suzanne and coming back to the set later. I take a video of us at dinner. Hang around the set and watch for awhile and leave. Come back at 6 a.m. to pick up Bo. Tell her that I would really like to work tomorrow and she said she would see what she could do.

February 11, Tuesday. I come in at 3 p.m. But I still can't be used tonight. They have scheduled me for some kind of fitting for tomorrow night at 6:30. So I get ready to leave and stop to visit with some people. Someone told me to get back into wardrobe, that there is an urgent phone call for me. It is my husband, he tells me that Dad is in the hospital. He is OK, but he has fluid in his lungs. He is awake and is eating. I inform the office, then leave to go home, don't know when I'll be back to the set.

I spend the next two nights with my Dad in the hospital. He can't be left alone because he won't settle down or stay in bed. He does fine, we talk a lot and I help when the nurses aren't there. He is able to come home on Thursday the 13th. Thank God that he is well again and that all worked out with production. I call the set and let them know that all is well. They tell me to get back down as soon as I can.

56

February 14, Friday

Have to be at the set at 10:30. We go to Ensenada today to do the "lifeboats at dawn" scene. We dress as usual and then have to ride those old school buses again. The trip takes about 45 min. It is an absolutely beautiful day. Crystal clear, not windy or cold. The coastline is incredible, but the ride down is scary. I just don't like the way these guys drive. At one point, our two buses start to race each other. We could see the drivers laughing, but we didn't think it was funny and start telling them to slow down. After several demands from us they stopped speeding and didn't do it again the rest of the trip. Can't believe the blatant and total disregard for our safety.

We arrive at the Corral Resort where our lifeboats wait for us. This is going to be fun. A nurse comes around with Dramamine and I take ½ a tablet. Deena, Shawn and I admire our lifeguards that are with us. One of the men says they're gay, we look at him and say "you're just jealous." We later discover that the guards are best friends and have wives waiting in San Diego. We try to arrange ourselves in the boat, but they have too many rocks in the bottom of ours. That's right, they put the rocks in the lifeboats for ballast. There are also too many dummies (not us) these are life size dummies that have been used as "fill" for people. They are all over the set and many times have been placed in odd positions with pants down and skirts pulled up. What can I say, people get bored and do many things to entertain themselves. This was not over-looked by someone in the crew when they discovered the dubious positions on deck after shooting one night. This caused a warning to be issued to us in writing from the office, that if we got caught messing around with the dummies, we would be fired. Now that statement provoked the response from one of the men…"what do they mean by messing around?" and that spurred a number of conversations, which are not suitable to be written here. Suffice it to say it was extremely funny though.

So we get out and wait for all that to be taken care of. We provide much entertainment for the tourists that have gathered around. Little do they know of the history in the making that they have the privilege to watch. We line up and give them a leg shot to photograph, then it's back to the boats we go. There are four of them at the dock, surrounded by all kinds of modern-day boats and yachts. This really looks strange, like something from the Twilight Zone.

In our boat we have Bo (our AD), Shawn, Dario, Doug, Maria, Ester, Diego, Katherine, Bob and Deena, who is with me in the bow. We start out, being pushed and pulled by the Zodiac boats. There are many people waving and video taping us from their boats as we pass. This is quite a parade for such a beautiful evening at sea. On our way out, Maria asked me how we knew if we were getting seasick. I told her you get hot and you start to drool. We all laugh at that and enjoy the ride out as I tell of a trip we took to Catalina and the dog that got seasick on that journey.

It's not choppy, but the swells are big, at least 6 feet and there are a lot of them. We go out at least a half a mile to an area where the camera barge is. By the time we get there, who do you think is getting sick? Me! Deena keeps telling me to look at the horizon. I tell Bo to have the nurse bring the other ½ of that pill out for me. She looks at me and says, "Oh no, you're kidding, right?" I replay "No, I'm not!" She calls for the nurse to come out and Harry brings her. He is laughing at me, saying

"I thought it was going to be you." I just tell him "Shut up man, just leave me alone, don't pick on me or I'll puke on you!" The nurse tells me that a pill won't work now because it will take to long. She needs to give me a shot so it will work faster. In order to do that, she must get into the boat with us. Everyone is laughing, because I think I'm getting the shot in the arm, but nooo, I have to get it in the butt! Now, they really start in and out come the cameras. No shame with this group, we've been together to long. I pick up my skirt and drop my many layers of tights to expose the upper half of my cheek and give everyone a Kodak moment. To say the least, I was the center of amusement for everyone tonight. After that, I curl up in the bow and pray I don't puke. Not so lucky are some others in the other boats. We hear that four lost it in one and someone else was so bad they had to be taken to the barge. Ah, what a life. The sunset is beautiful, the moon and the stars start to come out and here I am, sick! We finally get the boats set and we are in position for about four takes. That's it, we're done and we start back in. I feel a little better, but still queasy. Bo keeps calling out to me to see if I'm still alive. "Hey, Jude, you OK? Never seen you so quiet, you worry me!" As we get back to the docks and calm water, I feel a lot better. I definitely don't feel like eating though. It's back in the bus for a cold ride back. Arrive at the set by 9:30 p.m. I find Ellen to get the hotel key from her. That shot really put me under, can hardly keep my eyes open. Walk into wardrobe and there is a message for me from home again. Dad is back in the hospital, but there is no way I can possibly drive home tonight. I call to make sure he is OK, he is resting comfortably and not to worry. Ellen is on the Carpathia set and doesn't get back to the hotel until about 5:30 a.m. I sleep until 10:30, then get back home by 1 p.m. Find out that Dad still has fluid in his lungs. I stay with him again and he is able to come home Sunday morning. I call the set and I'm told I don't have to go back to work until Friday. It's good to be home for the next few days.

57

February 21, Friday

Get back to the set at 9 a.m. Everyone is asking about my Dad, if he is OK. Find out that the schedule had changed and I didn't need to come in today. They didn't cancel me in time so they give me ½ a days pay. I hang out for a while to get paid from the other day. Chucho (the man with the money) is busy so I have to wait about an hour. While I'm waiting I try to straighten out the mix up on my wet suit. They had placed the wrong one on the rack with my outfit. No luck in getting that done today. I get paid and leave for awhile. Go dress up a little and come back to apply for a painting job on the set. Find out it is too late in the shoot and that they are already laying people off. I visit with Zubie for a while and then finally get to go to dinner with Ellen, Suzanne and Linny at El Patio. Linny has some new "Titanic" shirts, so I get three more. Good stuff for all of us to have!

February 22, Saturday. Still no work, I should have gone home last night, I guess. I moved out of the beach house again and try to get the key to the hotel to stay with Ellen. She is on the Carpathia set and I can't get to her. So I hang back and just wait. This is a set that is located just next to the Titanic. It appears to be the full size upper deck from the funnel, the bridge and the forward Well Deck of the Carpathia. There is not enough room to build another ship. This is where the survivors were first gathered after being rescued from the lifeboats. Unfortunately I only get a glimpse of this set and can't be sure of details. They wrap early, about 8 p.m. so we all go to dinner at El Nido. Had the best shrimp dinner there and totally pigged out. All the stunt people are there, so we sit with Laurie, Dave, Franklin and Jay. Go to the Rosarito Beach Hotel and then to Rock 'n' Roll Taco. We are told that we missed the show, that Billy Zane was there and jumped into the swimming pool. The pool is apparently closed this time of year. He was arrested and taken to the station. After they found out who he was, they brought him back. We never did hear anything about it later and don't know how true it was. It was fun, but I'm not into the night club bit, I guess. To bed by 3:30 a.m.

February 23, Sunday. Go to lunch with Ellen at 1 p.m. Go get Bo, who rented a house five miles north of the set, at 2:30 and find her still in bed. Finally get her moving and leave to go back to Rosarito at 7 p.m. We go to El Minido for drinks and appetizers. Then to El Nido again for the shrimp dinner. This time the prop people are there. Have a good time and then we go to Bo's landlord's house and sit in their redwood hot tub. We talk about everything that we can think of, family and things that we've done. We stay there until 1:30 a.m. I stay at her place tonight. She has no heat and it is freezing. Glad I had my sleeping bag, but it was still hard to sleep.

February 24, Monday. Have to take Bo and her dogs to San Diego. Her dog had fallen and dislocated her rear leg and it was time for the vet to check it and take off the bandages. After the vet and all checks out well, we grab some lunch and head back to the studio. Get back at 2:45 and find I have no call again. I pack up and go home.

February 27, Thursday. Get called at 9 a.m. to be at the set by 3:30 p.m. I hurry and get packed and on the road. I arrive on time and dress 3rd Class. We are supposed to do Collapsible A, but it is very windy and cold. I am not feeling well. Last weeks treatment only slowed a nasal infection. Because of the weather, they wrap us at 1 a.m. Glad I did not have to go out in the cold. I just go home and get warm.

February 28, Friday. Get up early and go to town to get a different antibiotic. Then to the set at 3:30. Our call has been canceled because something is majorly wrong with the ship. I see Zubie's assistant and ask what is wrong. He said that one of the support legs has collapsed or something to that effect. I see a couple of people on my way out, visit a bit and head back to the house. I still don't feel good, so I stay the night again.

February 29, Saturday. Go to the set at 3:15 p.m. and there is no one there at all. Everyone has the day off. Can't find Ellen, guess she went home too. Find out the ship will be dead for at least a week. Go get Bo and take her and the dogs back to my house in San Marcos for the rest of the weekend. A couple of the stokers want to come over and take Bo out for the evening. Later, they come back and get in my spa.

March 1, Sunday. We all get together and go to our favorite restaurant for breakfast, Grandpa Allen's, in San Marcos. Have a great time talking and telling everyone what has been going on down in Mexico. Later that night we go to dinner at some other friends from the set, the Kosty's. We have a very nice dinner and evening at their house. Bo will go back to the set with them on Monday.

March 5, Wednesday. Get called in to be on the set at 3:30. Finally, supposed to do Collapsible A. The ship is separated in half now. Cut between the second and third funnels. Repairs to the hydraulic system and supports must have worked. We are on the set four days sooner then we thought. The front of the ship is now called the "riser." It can be lowered and raised in the 45 foot deep tank that it is suspended in by huge steel cables, three on each side and each cable is 2 inches in diameter. I still can't believe the planning and engineering that has gone into this set. Another great thing they have done is at the edge of the front of the tank where it becomes shallow clear over to where the bow used to be. At least a couple hundred feet. They have painted part of the forward Well Deck and bow on the blacktop under the water, so it will appear to be there, as the ship is sinking. They have even put some bubble making tubes around where the big cargo hatch is. It looks great and with the water covering it, no one can tell the difference. We never do anything tonight and we wrap at 6:15 a.m.

58

March 6, Thursday

Get called to the set at 3:30 p.m. We get up on deck at sunset. Hurry up there to just sit around and wait. Finally, do some more "crowd crush scenes." We do get to do this about 7 times. Things seem to go really slow tonight. It's cold and wet again. We keep ourselves stashed inside as much as we can. We find out that the stunt people have taken our places in Collapsible A because there is a big struggle staged for that shot. A lot of fighting will take place to get into the boat and some of the women are thrown out. It is boring just watching this and we wish we could be where they are. We all joke that they don't want us to get hurt (which they don't) and I tell Si that I want to do my own stunts, so her services aren't needed for me. She laughs and says "OK", as she heads back to do more shots.

As time passes, Mr. Cameron comes by and says "Hi" to me again. It has been nice that he and all of our other "bosses" acknowledge us when they see us or go by. They now change scenes and some of us get wrapped at 5:15 a.m.

March 7, Friday. Back again at 3:45 p.m. We do some more scenes for Collapsible A, but mostly do nothing all night. They are sinking the set now. A lot more than the last two nights. We are able to go up on the back half of the Observation Deck and watch how everything is being done. It is incredible how this huge set is being lowered into the water. The way the water rushes up the deck and over the railing in front of the bridge, it just looks so real and frightening. As I stand and watch the stunt crews at work, hear their screams and watch the struggle of all that are on deck, it sends a chill down my spin. I feel it, just like I did when lifeboat 14 comes back to look for survivors. How my heart aches. If I didn't know that this was make believe, I would be trying to rescue people. The tears flow freely as once again fantasy depicts a long ago reality for a struggle to survive.

March 8, Saturday. Get to the set at 3:30 p.m. It is nice and warm tonight, another Santa Ana seems to be developing. We get our 6 mil wet suits on and are up on deck about 7:30. Sebastian sets us up, he has Ellen and I half way up the deck. We are to run to the side, look over, see what is happening at the lifeboat, run to it, then when the water gets to us we run back up the deck. The first time that we do this, we don't get wet. Our thought was if we don't have to and we can out run the water, why not stay dry? Well, Sebastian is quick to point this out. We laugh about it, but he wants us to get wet! So we get wet…just a little bit more!

Now it is time for dinner. Crappy again. Glad I continue to bring my own. Even our craft services has reverted to its usual bad selection. Thought that with only a few weeks left, things would stay good. When we were on the inside set it was excellent. Don't know what happened.

Back to the set and pick up where we left off. The shot gets set and we go again. This time, we get wet to our knees. Not uncomfortable at all. I really didn't need the thick suit, because it is so warm out tonight. Sebastian is much happier that we have gotten wet. I guess he didn't feel so alone. We also meet some of our lifeguards that are from San Diego-Frank, Pat, Larry, Paul and Scotty just to name a few. We all hit it off right away and have a great time. These guys are great, they all get assigned four people to take care of. Larry is in charge of our group. We are to keep an eye on each other and make sure that he sees all of us after each take. Finally wrap at 5:30 a.m.

59

March 9, Sunday

I stay in Rosarito with Ellen. I just want to get in on a couple of parties before it all comes to an end. I pick up Bo and go to dinner at El Nido. We end up meeting Ellen, Suzanne, Gemma, Carrie, Yvette, Paublo, Diego and some others having dinner. Sebastian and his wife show up and sit with us, too. We start talking about tricks that we would like to pull on people. I would really like to find out where Mr. Cameron is staying and T.P. it. I wonder what reaction we would get as I hear he is staying in a private villa. That is if Schmitty didn't shoot us first! Sebastian wants to put a blow up doll in Josh's place. Never find out exactly why. Short sheeting, corn flakes in the pillow case and plastic wrap over the toilet were discussed as well. Oh, and don't forget to put tooth paste on the toilet seat, too!

After dinner, Bo and I go to the set. We watch some of the stoker scenes get shot. This is a really neat set. It is set up in one of the out buildings. They are using real coal, so that makes it really dirty. It looks like they have four to six boilers, which the men are working. Lighting is set up inside the boilers to simulate the fire. It is not easy to see everything, because there is a high wall around the set so they can flood it. On action, we can hear the doors open that release the water. The men start screaming and panic ensues as they clamor to escape. From where I am I can't see. It is eerie to listen to this, because they sound so real. The steam hissing, the metal crashing as the doors to the boilers slam shut and water tight doors close down on the men that can't escape. Then we hear "cut" and laughter fills the set as everyone settles down and realize it is a good take and everyone is "OK".

Now we leave and head for a party at Club Marina. We stay for a couple of hours and I watch a lot of people get hammered, almost everyone smokes, but it is fun to be able to talk to people that we don't normally get to see on the set. As I am mingling, Bo disappears. I start asking people if they have seen her. I go outside to find her in one of the hot tubs. With her clothes on! I finally get her out and help her to my Suburban. As we are leaving, we see Jason (who plays Tommy) and a stuntman named Craig, wandering around like they are lost. Apparently they missed their ride and were stranded. We load them up in my truck and take them back up to La Paloma Hotel. They are very grateful and I get them to sign my journal before they leave. Drop Bo off at her place and then go back to meet Ellen and Suzanne. Finally get to bed at 4 a.m.

March 10, Monday. Have to get up at 9 to take Ellen up to the toll gate area on the main road for her car. It broke down again and she has to have it towed back to San Diego. After that and making sure she is ok, I go back to the house and sleep a couple more hours. Get to the set at 3:30 p.m. I put on my thinner wetsuit because it is another beautiful Santa Ana night and it is warm. As we set up for the same thing that we did on Saturday, Simon asks us who his strong swimmers are. He wants us to jump off the side of the ship and swim away! They are sinking the set even deeper now. We get into our groups with our lifeguards, there are about 15 now. As the set sinks, I go to the edge of the deck and try to jump, but the water comes up too fast and I am just able to push off the edge. It is a very creepy feeling, I can feel the suction of the ship as it is going down. There is a bubble machine just in front of me and it keeps me from moving away as fast as I would like. I finally kick free and make it to the edge of the tank where it is only three feet deep. When we reach this point we are to continue to look like we are in deep water. This is not hard for me, but the tall people have to fake it a little more. I'm able to see the Collapsible action from a different angle out here. It also brings me a little closer and I can see more. All I can say is "Wow," the stunt people are awesome. I thought it looked frightening before, but now even more so. On "cut" we stand up, look for our lifeguard and people, and give a "thumbs up." We stand there for a few minutes and then they tell us to go to the warming tent. In order to get there we have to walk across the rest of the tank, about 100 yards or so and also step over the cables that raise and lower the ship. No one can move until the set is locked off and secure. If we go past a certain point of safety we will be fired! These cables could do some damage if you got caught in them, like "lose a limb" type damage.

We get to the warming tent and there is a huge heated spa waiting for us. There are also some heaters placed around the seating area. We are able to get warm in the water and then get out and sit. Most of us take our costumes off and then we can take down our wet suits to dry off a bit. We break for dinner, and tell of our excitements during the filming that we had just finished. Apparently, the left side of the boat house collapsed inward and sucked a couple of our people in with it. They were OK but as can be imagined, quite shaken. Being the troopers that we are, they were back for more after dinner. We do the same thing and it goes well. Wrap at 5:30.

60

March 11, Tuesday

To the set at 3:45. Get dressed with my light wetsuit on, big mistake. In the water to much and can't wait to change. I was getting cold and was trying to stay out of the night air as much as possible. I stand in the doorway that leads to the inside of the boat house. Sebastian sees me in there and asks me what I am doing. I told him that I was cold and just trying to get warm. He has to wear this big black jacket during filming so he blends in. He takes it off after each take (about 5 times) and gives it to me to wrap up in. That was really nice of him. He has always watched out for us, but this is special to me. I couldn't thank him enough. In between takes one of the special effects guys named Jay comes out and heads to the ladder to climb up to the top of the boat house. As he is moving up the deck, something happens and he takes a nasty fall. He is down for a couple of minutes. Some of the crew help him off the deck. He really hurt himself, but we don't know the extent of his injuries. As we are gathering for a different shot, I stand up on one of the lifeboat cradles and look around for someone that is in our group. All of a sudden, I slip and fall flat on my side. Stunned for a moment, Sebastian was right behind me. He bends down and starts to help me up. Everyone around me gets quiet real fast and asks if I'm OK. I'm not hurt, just wondering how I did it and feeling totally stupid, I thank everyone for helping me. After splattering myself on the deck, we go overboard again and I am able to place myself in a better position to get away from the ship. We get cold tonight and to the tent we go as soon as possible. After dinner, I change into my thick suit and end up just sitting in the spa the rest of the night. I go out on the berm near the tank a couple of times to watch the stunt people work the rest of the night. Wrap at 6:30 a.m. As I undress, I notice I have a small bruise on my right hip from my spill on the deck, but I don't care. I just didn't want Jay to feel so alone. We can compare bruises when he comes back.

March 12, Wednesday. Get to the set at 4. Things are starting to wind down now, it's hard to believe, but there is only about 2 weeks left. I put my thick suit on tonight and sit around until midnight. Then I am told to go get dressed in my 1st Class outfit so I can get back into boat 12 again. What a bummer, now the lifeguards can't save me anymore. I sit around on the berm just watching everything that is going on out on the set.

Now there is nothing else exciting going on the rest of the night, so I can tell of one of the most exciting things of the movie so far. As I was sitting in the hair department tonight, April says "Arnold (Schwarzenegger) is here!" I say "Ya, right." She's serious and says "Look!" I turn around to see him. He is on the other side of the room, making his way around to our side. I am the only one at the end of the row. He walks right over to me, bends down, two feet from my face and says "How are you?" I say "I'm fine." Now, do I reach out and shake his hand? No! I just stand there stupid and melt into the floor. I could have shook his hand and I am frozen with shock that the one person I have wanted to meet for so long on this set is now right in front of me and I can't move or talk! He walks away and all any of us can do is follow him around like little kids. Trying to get were I can shake his hand again, but to no avail. I call home and report and no one can believe I reacted that way. So shoot me now! Wrap at 6, to bed by 7 a.m.

March 13, Thursday. To the set again at 4 p.m. I dress 1st Class. Head out to the berm to load the lifeboats. I try to stay on land as long as possible and run to use the restroom just before heading out. I have on plenty of clothes to stay warm and even bring an extra jacket for in between shots. Pack our pockets full of goodies, we have a feeling it's going to be a long night. The Zodiacs pull the boats out to an area next to the ship. They put us in position to do the gondola scene. That's when 10, 12, 14 & Collapsible D come together just after the ship goes down. Boat 14 transfers it's passengers to the other boats so it can go back for survivors. This is where they discover the man that is dressed like a woman. After he is found out he is thrown into one of the other boats. We do this several times and it looks very impressive.

Around the outer edges of the set large black screens have been erected. They are either there to block the lights from the road or to keep people from photographing the set. Anyway, they are fairly tall, maybe two stories and there are some special effects guys up there. They have some large smoke machines and it appears they are trying to fog the set. The wind is not cooperating and it is blowing the smoke away from us. With the way the lighting is set up this gives a very eerie effect. The men's shadows are being cast on the smoke and they look 3D. After we do this a few times, it is time to change shots. They have to take a few of us out on the Zodiac because our weight causes us to be to low in the water and the lifeboats can't clear the cables. This is fun, we narrate the trip like the Jungle Cruise at Disneyland. The rest of the night, we goof around with the lifeguards and everyone else. We watch the swim crowd, this is a special group of extras that have been brought in just for the large crowd scenes after the ship goes down, there about 250 of them. This is all they do for the rest of the night. After some time we wrap at 5:30.

61

March 14, Friday

Back to work by 4. Dress 1st Class and get ready to do more of what we did last night. End up doing nothing, but sitting around watching and talking. It appears that they get stuck on the set that has been built along side of the tank where the Poop Deck sat. It is an "L" shaped hallway that has three large overseas containers filled with water at one end. The other end points down the driveway toward the ocean. The containers are elevated and tilted down to a ramp that channels the water into one end of the hall. When the water is let loose it crashed through the doors and rushes like a raging torrent until it reaches the other end. It's like flushing a pull chain toilet, the kind that has the tank a couple of feet above the bowl. It's really fun to watch, because what ever and who ever is in there comes out on the other end and rolls out onto the driveway. The Titanic water slide has been born. Now we can have a theme park, too! Titanic, The Ride, but we don't get to use it. This is an exclusive, made just for the stunt team. Wow, we could have things like The Poop Deck Tilt-a-Whirl or Let-U-Go

Lifeboats, The Funnel Fall, The Tumbling Deck, The 90º Plunge of Doom, The Stairway to No Where, The Rat Run, The Common Room Dance of Torture, The North Atlantic Ice Plunge and the Rise-N-Fall of the Titanic Empire! I let my mind go nuts until we wrap at 5:30.

March 15, Saturday. Get to the set again at 4 p.m. Dress 1st Class and have to redo the lifeboat scenes, because some of the cameras were not focusing properly. We do that a couple of times and that takes about an hour. Next I go change into 3rd Class and wet suit. We go out and do two scenes on the riser (sinking set) again. That takes another hour. It's time for dinner, which has gotten worse. I know that I said I must stop this but I must make note that it has really reached the bottom of the barrel now. Last night they had tongue and tonight they put out liver. We suspect that tomorrow night will either be brains or tripe and then our last night will be the crowning glory of kidney's and mountain oysters, which would go along very well with the royal screwing that we have gotten from these caterers. I'll get off my soapbox again and back to the business at hand.

I go shower off and change back into 1st Class again. My hair is in total chaos and the make up is dead white. We are to look like we had a very rough night in the lifeboats, as we board the Carpathia the morning after the sinking. We wait around and I never get into that scene. Have a good time with Bo watching them film this part and raiding the crew tent. Wrap at 6 a.m. Get some sleep, pack up and head back to San Marcos.

March 17, Monday. Went home for a day of rest and get back today at 4. As I enter wardrobe, I quickly discover that Bo had been robbed of $3000, early on Sunday morning before we went home. Nobody saw anything and there isn't anything anyone can do. Also find out that someone else had her whole week's pay taken from her. We just have to be very careful with what we have. A collection of $150 was taken and given to Bo to help a little. I think the gesture meant the world to her and she cried.

Dress in 3rd Class, but no wetsuit tonight. As we get on deck, a few of us are asked to go topside. They want us to be stand-ins for ourselves as they set the shot. It's freezing, plain and simple. Even with the two layers of thermals and two of tights it is a piercing cold. We all go and reinforce our clothing as we get a chance. We wait around a lot. They are getting ready to "break" the ship in two. Not at all how I thought it would be done, but it still looks really cool. The deck has been cut and set with balsa and real wood veneers, like paneling. These products are used because they are flexible and they will splinter and buckle like the real deck, but without as much pressure to make it happen. There is some kind of hydraulic mechanism under the deck that lifts and pushes the two sides apart. They have placed a look-a-like facade in front of the deck house that splits apart. It is connected to the hydraulics and moves with the deck. The railing has been set so it will break away and stunt people fall through onto pads that are on the deck below. Smoke pours out of the break, a strobe light and sparklers provide the electrical short effects. Now we take our places for our part. I am with a group of people that are to look like we are hanging from one of the deck benches. We have to lay on the deck to give the effect that we are at a 45 plus degree tilt. We are now ready. On "Action" I can't see how the effect looks, but I can hear it. Crunching, grinding, snapping and sizzling. Sounds great! We get to watch the reset and the stunt people climb out of the hole. After break, we only have enough time for one more shot. I think this has been one of the most time consuming effects, 14 hours and only two shots. We wrap at dawn.

62

March 18, Tuesday

Have to be at the set at 3:45. In 3rd Class and wetsuit, ready to go by 5. Hurry up and wait, we sit around doing nothing until they wrap us at 1 a.m. What has gone wrong tonight? Find out that the generator for the riser has died, big time.

I end up taking Vanessa (from hair) and her boyfriend on a walking tour of the ship. All the camera crews have moved to the labyrinth on the inside set, so we can take our time sight seeing. The first thing we visit is the breaking set on top. It is taped off so we can't get very close, but we are able to see quite a bit. I tell them how it all seemed to work but, I can tell they want to be alone so I say my good nights and head on over to the inside set. I try to watch some of action there, but can't see anything. It's been kind of sad today. People are getting wrapped and sent home. Ellen left too, but will come back on Monday to reshoot Ensenada. That's right, found out that the cameras weren't operating properly that whole evening we were in the lifeboats and they have to go back to do it all again. That is a huge cost to take everything back down there.

March 19, Wednesday. Get to the set at 4 p.m. Find out that Vanessa's boyfriend proposed to her last night up on deck. How sweet, they will never forget that. To my knowledge no one else has done that here. What a memory and story they will have to tell later on in their lives together, that they got engaged on Titanic!

Dress in 3rd Class and wetsuits again. We have to get on the set a little differently tonight. They have removed the gang way, so we can't get on the riser the usual way. We get to go, what they call the "back way," down below under the ship. I love it, it's like we get to explore where no extra has gone before! We go through the walkways that access the lower parts between the two halves of the ship. Out into the water, around one side to the deck and step up on the boat deck. The set is deeper into the water than before. I end up standing on the rail to avoid long exposure to the water. I slip and fall into the water a couple of times and that keeps everyone smiling. As the cameras roll we jump or swim away again. Then after we do this a couple of times, we change positions. During these takes they had arranged explosives in a couple of areas to give the effect of cables snapping as the funnel falls. They look like they are strung on some type of cable or rope. They are loud and impressive. We had to be careful not to go near where these charges were set. Simon tells us that they could cut us in half. Once again, if you cross that line of safety you're out.

After break it's back on deck. This time I'm up on top with Sebastian again. We are standing near where the 1st funnel had been removed (we think someone came and stole it with a helicopter the other night!) We do a few takes where we swim off to one side as they film the panic in Collapsible A. This is really a weird thing to have this huge set sink under you. It is a little different then before, because we are on the front and it really sinks deep into the tank. I try to hurry back so when they raise it I can ride it back to the surface. I'm having a great time. Then Sebastian asks me to go over to the right side and swim from there. I get to jump, about 5 feet down into the water from the top of the Wheel House. Then, I have to stay in deep water and cling to a window there. As he is telling me this I ask him why Lou and him get such a kick out of having me do weird things. It's Judy run, Judy jump, Judy hang. I tell him what Lou said about me being lively and all. He laughs and says "Well, you are!", so back to swimming I go.

I'm with a lifeguard named Joe. He lives in Ramona, graduated in '93, same year as my son Jeff did from San Marcos. We do what Sebastian asks a couple of times and then go back up front again. They are going to drop the funnel into the water from a crane. We swim out to the front mast (the mast is actually bolted to the concrete where they have painted the forward part of the ship) and on my way out I hear "Judy, go south (I go north) No, no you're going north, Judy go to the ship." OK, so I'm on my way back and I get caught in the big bubble machine and it pushes me west. "No, no honey, now you're going west. Judy go to the ship and take that group of people with you!" It is Josh and I can't see him. How did he pick me out of that crowd? Of course, this is being broadcast through loud speakers all over the set. This is really funny, because he can't hear that I do understand, I'm just stuck! Dying of embarrassment, a new title of "wrong way" is attached to me for a short time. I'm finally able to break the bubble grasp I'm in and get back to the ship with my group in tow.

They now get started with the funnel. Even though we are nowhere near it when it falls, it still is startling the first time. The crane suspends the funnel over the tank. It is not as big as the ones on the ship, but it is weighted with those concrete freeway dividers. The cable makes a snapping noise when it releases, the crane sways from the release and crash! This thing hits the water after a good 35 foot drop. It makes a good wave and pushes us around a little. We get to do this a few times. I have fun tonight, the most for awhile. Time does go by when you're having fun and it ends too soon. Not for some though, they got a bit cold and had to warm up, but they were fine. We go to wardrobe and I find Bo shivering, her feet and hands are like ice. She spent too much time in the cold water without a break. We call the doctor down to make sure she is OK. He checks her over and she almost has to go to the doctor's trailer. We bundle her up, wrap at 6:30 and I take her home. I turn on the heater, pile the blankets on and she falls right to sleep. She will be fine, just needs to rest now.

63

March 20, Thursday

Don't have to be to the set until 5:30. Dress 3rd Class, now waiting to be used by second unit. Say good-bye to more of our friends that aren't needed any longer. Do a lot of walking around the ship, looking at all the destruction to our proud beauty. Another gal named Judy and I take a hike around the ship again. I take her up on deck to show her around. She had never been up there before. I feel like a tour guide and have fun doing it. Go sit some more, then the fog rolls in, heavier then I've seen it before. Never do anything the whole night and we wrap at 5 a.m.

March 21, Friday. Get to the set for what I believe is my last day. It is 5 p.m. We get out to the riser at dark, about 6:30 or 7:00. We must do some more scenes on the riser. More of the sinking and us swimming off. I stand on the roof of the Wheel House and we are able to play around the hole where the 1st funnel was. It is like a big Jacuzzi, because they have a bubble machine in it and it actually feels like warm air blowing up. Our group is on the far side, closest to the ocean. We are to swim off in that direction (west). I get on the deck, next to the first davit on that side of the ship. I can see the lights way down deep in the tank. I had never giving much thought to how deep it was before. I got to look straight down into that abyss and it sure was creepy. I thought to myself that it must have looked this way for real, but the feelings of those that it was happening to were far different then mine. I know that I'm safe and that if something were to go wrong, there were lifeguards and scuba divers to watch out for us. This thought combined for a feeling of eerie beauty that could only be explained by someone that witnessed it. As I could study the details of the ship lights in the dark water, water that was 30° degrees warmer then that of the actual sinking. My thoughts are that it looks like a negative, only with shades of green and gray. I grabbed hold of the cable that was strung between the davit arms and hung there. I could see even deeper into the tank. I could see the lights on the Promenade Deck shining through the windows. I could see the red light down on the bridge wing. It was too deep to touch but I did try when the set was raised again. This time I shift my position more forward. I actually stand on the bridge wing and look down. It is really dark, but some lights are still on and you can see down just below the Promenade Deck walkway above the Well Deck. I look back, up the side of the ship and follow the black paint line along the side. It cuts off, abruptly where the set is cut in half, only blackness from then on. Where it is black, it makes me feel dread and fear. Where it is lit, it makes me curious, wishing that I could take more time to explore this thing that has become a part of me and will continue to be the rest of my life. I savor every moment, knowing full well that this adventure will end at dawn. Now, it is time for us to leave. Walking off, I move slowly, studying all the details that are left. The set is a wreck. Holes have been cut and floors removed to allow the water to flow rapidly. The whole interior deck floor of what would be the entrance to the Grand Staircase, has been removed and replaced with a heavy wire mesh. The entire boat house wall has been cut away, because it collapsed and wasn't needed anymore. All of the instruments on the bridge have been removed. Those pieces will be preserved after they are used in the set where the water bursts through on Captain Smith. Now we are to go back in and dry off and wait to do some more scenes at 4:30 a.m. It is going to be a long wait for when we are needed again.

It is now 11 p.m. and Bo comes in and tells us to get dressed in our thin wet suits, then go to the indoor set. There are four men and I that wait to be used in some of the labyrinth scenes. As we are waiting we get the privilege of having a great dinner. I have lobster and sit on the staircase that leads down to the cargo hold. The car is down there and I get to examine it, quickly though. From what I know of it, the whole side can be removed for filming of the love scene. The lighting is cool and it casts dark shadows, especially in the corners and around the car. At first it all looked black, but as I got close I could see its rich maroon tone with black fenders and top. So I knew that it was the same car that was seen during the Southampton shoot. The walls of the hold are split where the iceberg hit and fire hose nozzles supply the water spraying in. All the cargo is stacked and thick robe netting hangs over the tops of each stack of wooden crates. I am alone down here, but I can hear Mr. Cameron and Josh upstairs directing what they're shooting now. Not wanting to get in trouble, I conclude my tour and head back up to the top of the stairs.

We still are doing nothing and I go up to get a cup of tea. Billy Zane is there, so I hurry down to wardrobe and grab my journal for him to sign. He is very happy to sign it for me with a nice note to go with it. I just can't get over how beautiful this man's eyes are. He is very nice, we visit for a bit about the films that he has done. I told him that I loved "Tombstone" and that I thought it was a very underrated film. He seemed a little surprised and thanked me for saying so. He also told me of how lucky it was for him to be on "Back to the Future", kind of like being in the right place at the right time. He told me that he was just an extra on that set and got picked to be in "Biff's gang." I told him how I felt about being on this set and he told me to keep up my ambitions, you never know. We shook hands and said good bye and I watched him leave the set.

We are still wandering around, trying to amuse ourselves. They have moved the cameras over to the other set where Mr. Cameron is doing some filming of Kate and Leo on the bow. It is the bow that was on the exterior set. They have brought it inside. There is a beautiful painted sunset. Someone says it was an actual sunset that happened one evening outside when they were filming the same scene. As we are waiting around on this set, I see Russell Carpenter, our cinematographer. I told him how much fun I have had working with everyone, how I admired his patience and I appreciated how nice he has always been to me. He always seemed calm and laid back. He just kind of laughed and said he didn't have time for anything else. He introduced me to his wife, Patricia and the rest of the people that were in their group. I was shocked that he would do that. I felt honored that I had made such an impression on him that he would want me to meet all these people. I told his wife what a wonderful experience this had been for me and that Russell helped in my appreciation of film making. A bit later, she came back over to me and said that they were leaving and that it was a pleasure for her to have met me. Even a couple of the people that were with her said good night on their way out. I felt all giddy inside, I hope it didn't show too much. It was hard to stay subtle. I hoped that they would really remember me.

    I have now been asked to go back and dress in my heavy wetsuit. I'm to ask Sarah to try to get a different outfit and head out to Sebastian, who was waiting for us on the east berm. Sarah and I hurry to the back room, where she finds a different top and shawl. These are really nice and I said, "We should have found this outfit first," she kind of laughs and sends me on my way. I have had the ugliest clothes this whole time and tonight I get nice ones. Out to Sebastian I go. He says "I should have known it would be you to volunteer for this." I just say "Of course, who else?" He apologizes that we have to walk out to the ship in knee deep water, so I say "So carry me then!" He says "Let's go." There is a camera platform out there and Josh is on top. They are going to shoot some scene with a lifeboat. Josh looks down, from about two stories up, and says, "Is that Jude you got down there?" Now, I have a shawl over my head and a new outfit. It reminded me of the night when he picked me out of the crowd of swimmers. How did he do that? Well, after a quick conversation between Josh and Sebastian, they decide to send me back, because they didn't want another woman in the scene. Apparently there weren't any on this particular lifeboat. They thank me for coming out and apologize that they can't use me. I just say "OK, but after all I did to look different!" We laugh about it and I ask Sebastian if I could come up to the office later and have him sign my journal. He said "Sure, I'd be glad to." I walk back to the berm slowly, turning around a couple of times to see what they are doing. I see a group of men in a lifeboat struggling to get close to the ship, which is now doubling for the Carpathia. I guess they are filming the boarding scenes for the morning after. Sad, I turn back and finish my last trip across this tank. I get wrapped about 6:30 a.m.

I say good-bye to all those that I have come to know. I walk out the back of wardrobe, so I can see how the set looks in the daylight. As I face the ship, to the left there is a pile of debris. I see some familiar pieces of the Poop Deck, some of the Southampton buildings, decking and other large pieces of the set. All that we worked on would soon be trashed. They have also started demolishing the ship, that beautiful duplicate that was so painstakingly recreated for this, what I believe will be a masterpiece of a film. What a shame. We kidded about it going to Laughlin and being made into a casino or moved to another part of the set and become a bed and breakfast right here. There was even a suggestion of it being reassembled by the Queen Mary. All that I see here will never happen again but, as the real ship, will never be forgotten.

I walk up the road, past the big sound stage, where the 5 million gallon tank is. They are building a second bridge, where Captain Smith will meet his demise. It is being made with a heavy steel frame, so it will not collapse on the actor that will be inside as the water breaks through the windows with tremendous force. The care that has been taken for these sets still amazes me.

I approach Mr. Cameron's motor home, hoping to catch him before I leave. I see Schmitty standing outside, he is taking care of business as usual. I also see Jon Landau, he is very happy to see me and finally signs my book. He asked if Jim had signed yet and I said no, but I was hoping to see him before I leave. He says, "Well, Jim is on his way out right now." I was finally in the right place at the right time. Mr. Cameron comes out and walks toward Jon and I. He is more than happy to sign as Schmitty looks on. I said to him, "Look he signed it almost like you did." Mr. Cameron said "Hey, I'm the one that called you his bloody dead chick first!" I can't believe the mind of this man. He called me that six and a half months ago and he remembers. With everything that he has on his mind, he remembered that! He shakes my hand and thanks me for all of my work. I tell him what a pleasure it was and to remember me when he does T3. He looked at me with a smile and very positively said, "I will!" I think to myself, boy I hope so, but we'll see come Oct. or Nov. when that project is supposed to start.

Feeling that I have completed my journal with these signatures, I feel better about leaving. I now go up to Sebastian's office with Bo. She is so glad that I was able to see Mr. Cameron before I left. She knew how much it meant for me to see him. Now, we gather, Sebastian, Bo, Kari, Yvette, Hugo and Rudy. We are all tired, Sebastian shows me that his "dry suit" isn't. After using it so much it has developed leaks and he never complained, at least that I could tell. I told him that he was lucky he didn't catch pneumonia. After, I get him and Hugo to sign, we visit and they have a couple of beers. Then Bo and I leave. I get my stuff from the house and drop Bo off at her place. I go home with all my treasures and can't wait to go to sleep. As soon as I get home I get a call from the set. They tell me that I need to be back down there, tonight, at 8:30 p.m.!

64

March 22, Saturday

They want me back tonight at 8:30. I said "Why didn't you tell me before I left this morning? But of course I will be back down!" They apologized and told me that I was specially asked for. The only ones that would have asked for me are Bo or Sebastian. This must be important and I get 2½ - 3 hours of sleep. Load up the truck again for at least a two day stay and then head back down. I get down there 45 minutes early and then discover that these scenes are not going to be shot until around 4:30 a.m. Sunday morning. There are about 30 of us waiting to see what this will be like. We are to work with the second unit. No one in the second unit knows me, so I'm thinking that I really wasn't asked for. They have us get dressed and wait.

I go out to where the action is. Everything is set up around the tank below the tilting Poop Deck set. This is the set that had all the cardboard boxes in it for the stunt people to fall into when we were shooting the 90° tilting deck scenes and now it is filled with 15 feet or so of water. Amy from wardrobe was out there with her parents. She was so busy that she couldn't spend much time telling them what everything was and how it worked. With nothing to do but sit and talk, it was my pleasure to become their tour guide. I don't remember how long I talked with them, it must have been at least an hour. I told them how long I had been there, what we had shot and how all the sets operated. I told them all the things that Amy had done for me and how I enjoyed seeing her all the time. They were really nice, I'm glad I could help out.

    I also get a chance to visit with Lucy, one of the stunt women from England that I got to work with. She is the stunt double for Kate in the shot they are working on now. I ask her to give Gary Powell my best and to tell him that I have missed him these past couple of months. She said that he got hired on another film. She thought that it was nice that I would remember him. I told her that I met him at the tank, six months ago in Tijuana and how we had fun picking at each other ever since. She thought he would appreciate me asking about him. Well, she must go now. They are doing the whirlpool scenes, where Kate and Leo get sucked down with the ship. The lighting in the pool gives it a green glow. The all infamous bubble machines are operating. From where I am standing, I can see the camera crew under the water. There are scuba divers in there for the actors to give them air. I also find out that the water is heated. I bet Kate & Leo appreciated that for a change. They had to be in cold water on the labyrinth set without the benefit of wetsuits.

    After watching that for awhile I decide to go inside. I change out of my wet suit and costume, no use in keeping everything on for the next six hours. I find a place to curl up for awhile and try to sleep. After about 45 minutes, Yvette wakes me up and we all get to go to dinner at Deluxe (that is where the good stuff is). I sit with Julian and Alex, also Amy and her parents. I pig out, after all it is our last meal you know.

    With all this waiting around I take advantage of the situation and get some other signatures that I thought I had missed out on, Kirk and Chuck to name a few. I go to different places to see if I can see inside the tank a little better, but there is just too much stuff around to get close.

    Finally, the time has come. We are told to get dressed and get to the riser. To my shear delight, I discover that Sebastian had taken the second unit. He did ask for me and the others. He said he wanted people that knew what they were doing. Boy, did we feel proud. Jackie, Christina and I get the pleasure of being drug through the water by 12 life guards. We liked those odds and make it known that we do. We are on A Deck in the forward enclosed Promenade. We are screaming and trying to fight our way out of the rising water. Christina and I are together, she try's to go back to find her husband. I fight with her and won't let her go. The water over takes us and Scott runs to our aid. Scott and another life guard grab us and drag us up the deck, towards the camera and then off to the side, out of camera view. After each take, we clap and laugh and think of something different to do the next shot. This time I accidentally hit poor Scott right in the face with my open hand. Sebastian tells us to look into the camera, show fear and panic. That is not hard to do. The set sinks quickly and you can feel the water pulling you down as it over takes us running up the deck. The cameras are set up right at the end of the riser's deck where it has been cut in half. We get to do this four times and that's it. That was the most fun of all the nights in the cold water. It was definitely worth coming back down for. I wouldn't have missed it. Everyone agreed that it was great and the guys lavished us poor helpless women with praise. We were so jazzed and happy that we went out with a bang! Laughing and giving each other high five's and hugs as we return to wardrobe.

After getting dry and dressed we go out to watch some more filming. This really is my last night of being used in the film. I have my camera and book ready for signing by those that I haven't gotten yet, like Leo and Josh. I'm really after a picture with Mr. Cameron and there is only one way to do it, just ask. I am standing inside the interior set where they have moved to. Not paying attention to anyone except Mr. Cameron. He seems to be at a brief pause in the filming. Quietly, I edge my way over to him. When no one is speaking to him, I lean over and ask him if I can take a picture with him. He says, "Not right now, you'll have to wait." I say, "OK." He gets up to walk over to the set and then stops, turns quickly and asks me, "Do you have your camera here?" "You bet." I reply and pull the camera from my jacket, "I came ready." He says, "You're lucky, you're really really lucky, you caught me at the right time." I am ecstatic. Doug is nice enough to take the picture of us right there on the set. He gives me a pat on the shoulder and we say good-bye again. Sebastian was there and he thought it was great. Next, I get Leo to sign, he prided himself on how sloppy he writes. We all laugh, shake hands and he thanks me for being there. I also say good-bye to Kate. Now I find Josh. He is over by the goodie table and is glad to sign, he wishes me well and thanks me again for being there, too. After that, I see Julian over by the door. He can't believe that I was gutsy enough to ask Mr. Cameron for a picture. I just told him that I felt it was now or never, when could I possibly do it again? We leave the sound stage and see that a lot of things are being taken down. The tents that took such a beating in all the wind and rain are being neatly disassembled and packed in trailers. There are miles of electric cable that is being collected and made ready to go. The prop department is collecting all of the salvageable items that it can find. I leave slowly so I can say good-bye to all those that I missed yesterday. I hear from someone that the wrecking crew would probably start taking down the ship next week. They have to wait until the special effects people are done first. I see Zubie once more. I tell him how I will miss that bright neon green hat and his big smile. We wish each other well and I continue my trek to the front gate. There I say good-bye to all the guys that have greeted me everyday and said good night to me when I would leave for the past 6½ months.

I find Bo to tell her that I will not be able to go to Ensenada tomorrow for the reshoot. If I were to go I would have to stay another whole day for the effects of the Dramamine to wear off. That would be too much time away for me now. I must get home, too worried about my Dad and they really didn't need me. I told her that I would be back on Wednesday to pack her up and take her home. She told me that they would miss me, but that was fine and she would see me later. As I get to my truck I decide to take a drive down near the ship. I get some pictures of the piles of debris. I still can't believe that it is over. I drive out the gates and stop up the road a bit and get out on the running board of the truck. I look back at the ship once more and say a silent good-bye. My mind racing through the time spent here. Anticipating what it will all be like on the big screen. So many memories, so glad I kept this journal. Get home at 12 p.m. sleep.

THE LAST DAY
March 26, Wednesday

———◈———

I have to go back today to pick up Bo. I take my sons, Craig and Jeff. Also Craig's girlfriend, Francine whom I met on Christmas break. We arrive in Rosarito about 11 a.m. Stop at Bo's and wake her up so she can get packed. Stop and have lunch at El Patio at the Festival Hotel. This is where most of us stayed. It is very quiet now because everyone has been sent home. I think we will definitely be missed in town.

We go to the set once more. It is about 3 p.m. I need to drop off some of the clothes that I used which I forgot to leave the other night. I am able to see the wardrobe crowd once more and thank them for all their help that they had given us during filming. So much has changed in just three days. So much more has been destroyed. We see piles of what is left of the Grand Staircase, Dining Salon and the labyrinth sets. I guess not a lot could be done with it after the flooding scenes. We try to walk down to the ship, but it is roped off and we can't get too close. The ship looks like it is sitting way down deep in the tank. I've never seen it that low. I guess it looks this way because all the water has

Living the Legend: The Journal of a Titanic Background Actress

been drained out. We walk around the set and I see Kari still here. She had to stay to finish up with the second unit. I also see Scott, the life guard. He will be leaving to go home this afternoon. I apologize again for hitting him in the face the other night. He said it didn't hurt. Upon leaving I see someone else that I know from the construction department. He asked if I had heard the set fall. I asked him what he meant and he proceeds to tell me what happened about 2:30, just before we arrived. They had drained the tank and left this huge water logged set, unsupported. Only being held up by the cables that raised and lower it. Well with all buoyancy gone and at least a million pounds of steel and wood, the cables were not designed to hold and they gave way under the strain sending the set crashing down the last 30 feet into the bottom of the tank. He said the sound was incredible, like a freight train being derailed. Fortunately there wasn't anyone under it when it collapsed. I bet those that were around it ran, though. Now I know why it looks so low and why we couldn't go down to see it. We go back down, as far as we can to take a closer look. Somebody got the stupid award for that one. Upon leaving, we pass by a pile of chairs, dining room, steerage, patio and deck chairs. All left there for the trash, but we can't have any of them. That is so wasteful, I really would like to have gotten a couple of the steerage chairs. You would have thought that we would have been welcome to take it, but no, it wasn't allowed.

We head back to town and have a great dinner at El Nido again and finish off the evening with a bunch of fireworks that we bought. The bomber jets are the best. We light them, they take off and then explode in different colors.

Get to Bo's the next morning. Get her all packed and then have dinner with Shawn and her kids. We finally get home at 11 p.m. and sit in the spa. We reflect on what we have done. Share war stories from different sets that we missed being on. Bo will spend the next week with a couple of different people and then I will take her to the airport to go to her home to North Carolina.

It's all over, special effects will probably be working for another couple weeks, but we're finished. After getting my photos and autographs, I feel that I have completed one of the most exhausting and yet, rewarding things I have done in my life. I was ready for it to be over. I will miss

THE LAST DAY

so many and cherish each in my heart for the rest of my life. I dedicate this record to all of us that "didn't go down with the ship" and toughed it out to the end to become a part of this epic film and I am sure film making history. I hope the world appreciates the vision that brings this film to it. Remember, we are all human and this human loved the experience and what we will present to our fellow humans in December.

Now, in a tribute to those that built her, and died on the decks that sank with her.
To those that still live, we'd like to give, the world their story.
James Cameron style.
You be the judge. A most excellent adventure!

Extra's Premiere
December 17th, 1997

Finally our big day has arrived. Our "Extra's Premiere" is here. Outside the theater, we have the car that brought Rose to the dock and of course, many of us that were together for all those months during filming. We are all first class tonight! We are very excited to see how all of our hard work has come together. We had heard that there was something like 24 hours of editable film. No one knows what scenes will be used or the scenes that we might be seen in.

Don Lynch is there as a special guest and Bo Bobak asked me to deliver a message of "Thanks" to all of us that worked on the film, because she couldn't be with us.

As the movie began, we are all taken with the surreal scenes of the exploration of the ship and the music. We are all quiet through the beginning and then they get to "our" part…transported back to 1912, the ship, the boarding. It was none stop excitement for the next 3 hours. As we saw ourselves, there were claps and cheers. When we got to Ellen's "dead mommy with baby" scene we gasped, then clapped and cheered. I bet some folks that attended that night (that had no part in the filming) thought we were nuts, but hey, we knew what went into that and were glad to see the final results. No one except those of us that had worked on the film could understand. We all knew that seeing it together for the first time it would be like this. By the end of the film, there were tears and applause. We new we would have to see it again so we could concentrate on the story this time. I know that we were all very proud of what ended up on the big screen.

About the Author

In the years that have followed since the production of the film. I developed many new and great friendships with Titanic folks (mainly with those that are mentioned in the following passage). In October, 2000 my world was shattered by the loss of my son, Jeff. He suffered another aneurysm that he did not survive. He always told me to be happy, so I've tried. The opening scene of Titanic is especially touching for us as Jeff can be clearly seen waving good-bye standing in the middle of the Forward Well Deck as the ship leaves the dock. Extremely poignant for us in so many ways.

I went to college and earned my certificates for Digital Editing, actually inspired by Ed Marsh and a desire to make my own films. I have continued to be involved with many Titanic projects. In 2002, Mr. Cameron, Ed Marsh, Ken Marshall and Don Lynch picked me to be Molly Brown in "Ghosts of the Abyss." What a great honor that was! Especially after meeting Muffet Brown in '98 (Molly Brown's great-granddaughter) who told me that I have an uncanny resemblance to Molly herself. We all worked together and it was a fabulous time again in Rosarito Beach, Mexico, we actually filmed it in 7 days. My daughter-in-law, Francine joined us on that shoot, along with my good friend Ellen Mower O'Brien (the frozen dead mommy). I also brought along a young man that I had meet at college, Brett Sauey who played Sixth Officer Moody. To our surprise, there were several others that were in "Titanic" there, so it was like a little reunion. During that time we all worked very hard and long hours, with new technology 3D cameras that were developed by Jim and his brother, Mike. We worked entirely on the sound stages and green screens. Ken Marschall had many of his family members there, his sister Kat Lalore, her son Shane, his sister Elise Hicks and her husband William.

Jim had me do some adlibbing for Molly during a boarding scene, where I was telling those around me about my recent trip to Egypt and that a camel had peed on my leg. Then another scene where we were in lifeboat 6, he wanted me to stand up. Ok, well in order to do this, I had to step down into the bottom of the boat, it was about a foot lower then my feet could touch. I am only 5 feet tall, actually about 6 inches shorter then Molly. So we are hanging from our davit about 6 feet below the edge of the ship, maybe 10-15 feet above the floor of the set. Jim calls up and says "Judy, stand up." So I jump down into the bottom of the boat and disappear, all you could see from Jim's view point was my feather on my hat.... that brought the house down with laughter. Jim laughingly says "get her a couple of crates to stand on." I was also able to do my own stunts! While boarding boat 6, Molly was tossed into the lifeboat as it was being lowered, maybe 5-6 feet. I insisted on doing this and trusted everyone below me that they would catch me, they did and it worked great.

Don Lynch played Thomas Andrews and Ken Marschall played Bruce Ismay, it was amazing the resemblances these men had to the men they portrayed. During some down time, we were all in a theater that was built in the museum located on the set in Rosarito, waiting to be called in for the next scenes. We had been up for about 17 hours, in costume, dead tired, trying to sleep off and on and bored, very very bored. There was a podium in front of the room. So, here we are 1912 costumes and all and someone decides to get up and start telling jokes. We all took turns telling something, a story, a joke, you name it. Don, hands down was the winner. After that invigorating event, we were wrapped (done), changed into our street clothes and had a wrap party in the

About the Author

cafeteria…yes a real cafeteria was built, no tents, no crappy catering and it was furnished with all the tables and chairs from First Class, plus the food was GOOD! We also had paved parking lots! The set has certainly changed since it was built in 1995-'96.

In 2005, I got called to do "Last Mysteries of Titanic" where I played Molly Brown again. This was a 3 day shoot in Rosarito again. I went down there with Ken Marshall and Parks Stephenson this time. There we worked together on correcting some errors in design patterns with the chairs in the Turkish Bath. Ken and Parks also redid the Marconi Room. Ralph White, renowned ocean and Titanic explorer (whom we sadly lost in 2008) was there and portrayed Major Peuchen. Also in 2005, Lightstorm started work on a 10 year anniversary addition of "Titanic". Five of us "primary core extras" were invited to come and do interviews at Lightstorm. Our group, Ellen Mower O'Brien, Susanne Savilla, Allen Smith, Ken Rounds and myself. Sadly our interviews didn't make it to the final edition, but I was able to do some voice-overs for the "in the water" scenes and Ellen did voice-overs for make-up. We worked with Ed Marsh and Van Ling, the gentleman that played the Asian man that was in "Titanic". Ellen and I contributed to the photo library that was included in the special DVD release. While at Lightstorm doing our interviews, Jon Landau let us all take photos with one of Titanic's Oscars, while Don Lynch and Ken Marshall looked on. It was a fitting end to a very fun day.

Photos and commentary can be seen on Park's Stephenson's website: http://marconigraph.com/titanic/gota/gota.html

I hope this journal will preserve my memories for others to enjoy and be a part of the history of what it was like to be involved with the making of "Titanic" and that it will endure for years to come.

Printed in Great Britain
by Amazon